The Sad

Thankyou
for Sharing M J
Story B
Claine
T

Claire Rowden

The Sadder Side of Me

Claire Rowden

The Sadder Side of Me

This book is dedicated to my beautiful family.

Without you, I don't think I would have made it through.

Claire Rowden

The Sadder Side of Me

My Bell's Palsy Story

by

Claire Rowden

Claire Rowden

Trigger warnings:

This book explores suicide, grief and anxiety.

Front Cover Design

By

Jordan Hemmings

Claire Rowden

The Sadder Side of Me

One

It's always the worst things in life that sneak up on you when you least expect it. When you're plodding along, everything feels normal; kids are happy and healthy, work is good, and you feel genuinely happy within yourself; and then bam! It hits you, but not in an expected, obvious way; rather, it slowly and sneakily creeps up on you, changing your world upside down, shattering your happiness without you even realizing it is happening. That was how it was for me. I was happy, content with my daily life of being a wife and a mum to a busy household. I had even taken the next step and had decided to go back to work part-time now that the kids were getting older; I was waking up every day, taking life totally for granted, just like we all do. Blissfully unaware of anything bubbling beneath the surface.

I was, in a sense, completely clueless that both my mind and body were struggling and on the brink of distress. So, when this condition crept up on me, leaving me feeling physically deformed and emotionally broken, I didn't know what to do.

Over the years, I never have been able to handle stress too well, but I honestly assumed that what was happening to me was possibly a stroke or worse a heart attack, which confused me because I also assumed I was far too young for that to happen, being only thirty-seven years old. But no, one morning at around four am I awoke and sat up wincing with a sharp pain that was radiating underneath my left ear. I was tired after staying up late reading that night and I just assumed it was another throat infection on the way, which I was prone to suffering from a couple of times a year, so I didn't give it much thought, turned over and attempted to go back to sleep.

That following day I was at work, standing around in the crisp autumn playground supervising the children in my position as a mid-day assistant when I realized that every time the slight chilly wind caught my left ear it would cause a dull ache that was persistently getting worse, it wasn't a particularly strong wind, more of a breeze really but none the less it still made me winch, covering my ear to shield it with my scarf. Again, I didn't give it much thought other than to maybe make a mental note to call the doctors if it got worse, again still assuming it was just a throat infection and continued on with the rest of my shift. I watched mainly the year five group at lunch times and the banter I had with a few of the kids was something I looked forward to every day; you were not meant to have favourites, but it was hard when their comical cheekiness reminded you of your own kids.

The rest of my day continued quite uneventfully, I picked the kids up from school, took them home and began preparing the dinner followed by an evening of reading and listening to the kids chat about their day. By the time it came around to going to bed I still relatively felt ok, just a little off compared to normal, but as I mentioned before, I just assumed I had a cold or throat infection on the way.

The next morning, which would have been day two, I awoke again feeling pretty normal. I got the kids up, made my usual morning coffee in my extra-large mug, did my hair and makeup and got dressed. This time though, when I went into the bathroom and began to brush my teeth, I noticed the first significant change. The brushing my teeth part was ok but when it came to spitting the toothpaste out into the sink my mouth just didn't want to work properly, my lips did not want to purse together in the normal way that's required to spit out the paste, they just gathered in a bizarre way and the toothpaste fell out rather than was spat out. At this point I stopped and took note of myself. I watched myself in the mirror as I moved my mouth around, trying to work out what was going on and why I felt so weird and that's when I realised that the left side of my face was ever so slightly off, it just didn't sit right compared to the opposite side, and it didn't feel right either.

I didn't have time to ponder on what was going on, I never usually have any spare time in the mornings, and I didn't want to get myself all worked up in a fizz as I had four kids to get fed and had to make myself look looking respectable enough to get out the door for the school run; if you have teenagers then you will know that this in itself is a massive challenge, so I continued with my morning routine and pushed it to the back of my mind. I dropped my two eldest off at their senior school and then doubled back and dropped my two youngest off to the juniors before heading off to work.

Neither of the schools were close to each other, the senior school was a good twenty minutes' drive away, so I had plenty of time during driving back and forth that morning to secretly worry, I discreetly attempted to pull faces in the rear-view mirror to see what parts of my face were not working properly, also mindful that I didn't want to be late. After dropping off my two youngest it was always a sprint back to the car and a race to get to work on time as I literally had about a ten minute window, I worked at a primary school that wasn't too far from where I lived but traffic was a bugger in the mornings and considering it was my first job back after fourteen years of being a stay at home mum, I wanted to make sure I made a good impression.

My hubby, Justin was more than happy for me to stay at home and relax and read every day if I wanted to, but I felt that guilty pull of leaving the financial responsibility entirely on his shoulders. We had a largish family so we were never really very flush and could do with the extra income so when I saw the mid-day position I applied to get my foot back in the door. It wasn't long before I had moved my way up from mid-daying to working as a teaching assistant in a room full of four-to-five-year-olds, it was my dream job, the kids all had fascinating little characters and the group of girls I worked with in my class were all so lovely, we made a really great team.

Again, though that day at work my ear ached whenever the breeze caught me as I turned my head, and my face still felt wrong. It's hard to describe one side of your face not coinciding perfectly with the other, but that's how it genuinely felt. This sensation I hadn't felt before that seemed to prickle under the surface of my skin all along my left side. That afternoon I had promised to take the kids to McDonald's after school for a dinner treat, my mum came along for the ride as she usually did to keep me company and what I remember from those moments sitting in the restaurant wasn't of me making happy memories with the kids whilst we all ate a meal together, but one of pure paranoia. I would later realise this was the start of many moments like this. I knew my face was acting weird and not doing entirely everything that it should be doing whilst I talked and smiled but I put on a brave face for the kids and shared a worried look with my mum. I had chosen not to eat anything but instead went with just a strawberry milkshake instead; I wasn't up for eating as I was too worried and stressed about my face. When I struggled to drink my milkshake through the straw, again the pursing of my lips not cooperating as they should I initially panicked but forced myself to calm down and the only way I could do that was by making a joke about it to my mum. I was overly trying to see the funny side of the situation, to take some of the frantic worrying away and I knew my mum was doing the same, but when I looked up at the table opposite where we were seated I saw a small group of teenagers taking selfies and photos of each other, the phones were pointed in our direction and I instantly became paranoid that they were snapping a photo of the weird woman sitting on the table opposite with half a face that was wonky and wasn't considered the 'norm' which would leave me wide open to be ridiculed. I was convinced they were poised, ready to share a snap chat with all of their friends and have a good laugh at my expense. They weren't, of course. They didn't even know I existed, as teenagers do, they were totally wrapped up in their own world. It was just the beginning of a new paranoid state that I would soon discover would never leave me.

The Sadder Side of Me

Two

I have never been the most confident of women.

As a teenager I was forever on a diet of some sort or another, never confident within my own skin and always worrying what others thought of me, but as I got older, became a woman, a wife then a mother I gradually cared less about what others thought and started to be more confident in my choices. I wore what I wanted, regardless of whether someone else liked it or not. That doesn't mean I had a total overhaul. I still would not go on the school run without my make up on or without doing my hair, both simplistic tasks that shouldn't really matter if they were done or not but it was my daily armour that

I used to feel a little more confident, as far as I was concerned no one needed to see me in the morning without my face on, I would joke that if I did the kids on the school run would run screaming with fright if I didn't make that effort, or so I told myself anyway. Either way, in my mind if I looked nice and well-presented then I would have a good day.

But that armour wasn't working to well now. My shield was cracked and a distorted version of myself was peeking through. That evening, I managed to get a doctor's appointment to get my face checked out, after examining me she swiftly told me I needed to see a dentist not a doctor as it was probably an abscess on one of my teeth as she couldn't find anything physically wrong with me. luckily, I also managed to get an emergency appointment at my dentist, both only being five minutes away from each other. Shortly after leaving the surgery though I was left despondent, only to be told when I was lying there in the chair that there was nothing wrong with my teeth, everything looked fine and that I should go back to my doctor.

It was late by this point and I was getting slightly irritated and frustrated that no one seemed to know why my face and lips were not working properly, so I went home, sorted the dinner, and carried on with our evening as usual whilst trying to convince myself that if there was actually a serious problem then surely one of the professionals I had just seen would have picked up on it.

I gave my sister a phone call once the kids were in bed to voice my concerns, I explained what was happening and how I was feeling, just to verbalise my worries more than anything else and to have a bit of a moan about all the running around I was doing and that no one seemed to be taking my concerns very seriously. As she usually did, she talked me down from the ledge I was precariously balancing on and told me she would have a look to see what she could find out online.

When I woke up on the third day, I still felt relatively normal, thinking back now I didn't realise what had happened had even happened until I walked into the bathroom and looked in the mirror. I guess having just woken up my brain didn't register that something was seriously off. I walked the few steps from my bedroom into the bathroom, went over to the mirror and realized with devastating clarity that the entire left side of my face was gone. Paralysed from the top of my head all the way down to the base of my neck. I couldn't necessarily see a droop in the mirror, I was more horrified that when I spoke or tried to smile the left side of my mouth just stayed in the same flat line position. As you can imagine I was pretty freaked out, there was no point calling Justin as he was at work and if I'm honest I wanted to pretend it wasn't happening, so I carried on with the chaotic morning routine, fed and took the kids to school, keeping my face covered as discreetly as possible and talking as little as I could get away with so as not to freak the kids out. I kind of figured that if I didn't look directly at them then they wouldn't notice.

My nephew was in the same year at school as my daughter, so when I pulled up at the junior school and walked over to meet my sister as I usually did every morning, she instantly knew something was up. She knows me better then I know myself sometimes and always has her sister-radar on high alert whenever she can see that something is bothering me, even if I act like nothing is wrong, she always knew, even to the point where now I don't even try to pretend around her that I'm fine anymore, she doesn't give up till I tell her what's wrong anyway, which even though at the time I think I don't want to discuss my problems I might be having I always feel better afterwards for opening up. She knows this and is very good at it. It's just one of the things that make her such a good therapist in her daily job. I always said that I gave her all the practice she ever needed by having me as her little sister!

As I approached her on the kerb, I was hiding my face in my scarf and clearly had written all over my face that I was in full on panic mode.

'I'm freaking out Kelly, look at my face, it's totally paralysed, I don't know what's going on' I say this as I'm desperately trying not to cry, which is becoming increasingly harder standing in a street full of mums on their morning school run drop off. You would think that they would all be preoccupied with just getting their little ones into school, checking last minute water bottles are packed and lunch boxes haven't been forgotten, but anyone with a child of school age will know that this isn't always the case and playground drama, and gossip can be rife with some of the mums that love nothing more than to talk about someone else's misfortune.

'Claire, I think you really need to call 111, I think you might have Bell's Palsy'

'Bell's what? What is that?' In my mind I was panicking as I had spent most of the morning thinking that I was having a stroke, I had never heard of bell's palsy before, and this one threw me completely, but I was somewhat a little relieved to have another possibility other than that of a stroke, even if I didn't know what it was.

"I googled your symptoms last night and that is what kept popping up, it's worth a call just to be sure as there is a seventy-two-hour window for treatment." I was already on day three by this point and she had that tone to her voice that was fringed with concern, so I gave my sister a hug and said I was heading straight home to give them a call.

Three

I drove straight home and as soon as I got in, I threw my coat to one side and dialled 111. The lady on the other end of the call was absolutely lovely, I told her all of my symptoms and she also agreed it sounded very likely that it could be bell's palsy. She advised me to go straight to A&E as I was nearing the seventy-two-hour window for the viral medication to be successful.

My panic mode just upped a notch at this point. Luckily my mum was home, so I grabbed her on the way, and we headed off to get my face checked out. I was praying that this was going to be a quick fix, that they would send me home with some medication and I'd be right as rain by the weekend, but like all emergency rooms the wait was very long and boring, which led to lots of googling about my symptoms, a rabbit hole I knew I should not be dipping down but I had no restraint to prevent my fingers from their frantic swiping and tapping. I now know that my mum was also panicking on the inside, assuming the worst like me that I was possibly having a stroke, whilst playing it cool on the outside, she is good at that! Whilst I obsessively searched my symptoms it occurred to me that I might not have bells but there may be a chance that I might have Lyme's disease instead.

Three months previously I had been bitten by two ticks, both at the same time over the local field that was behind our house whilst trying to fetch the kids football out of the trees. I wasn't directly in the tree line but the grass along the edges of the bushes hadn't been cut and the grass was still quite long. As I was standing just inside the tall grass reaching up, I felt a sharp sting on the front of my leg. We never did get the ball down, but I had been bitten by two ticks, both had bitten me on the same leg a few inches apart. I did the usual, drew circles around them to make sure I could see how far the red area around the tick bites

27

grew and I contacted my doctor, after realising that one tick bite could be bad enough and I happened to have the luck of getting the twins of the tick world take a snack on my leg for the briefest of seconds that I happened to be standing in the long grass reaching for the ball! Once the doctor had checked me over, she advised me to keep an eye out for any symptoms of Lyme's, which frustratingly could take up to three months to make itself known. That would have roughly been around my time frame so on went more googling, even more panicking as the long-term effects of that could also be disastrous. But it wasn't long before I realized that not all of my symptoms were matching up, I had some that were similar but there were many that didn't go with how I was feeling. It was at this point my mum took away my phone, handed me a strong black coffee from the vending machine and told me to just wait and see what the doctors had to say. So, we sat, and we waited.

The chairs were typically uncomfortable for what you would expect from a waiting area, and the room was almost full to the brim of people all needing medical attention. I kept my head down as much as possible, trying not to make eye contact with anyone, if I wasn't attempting to talk to mum, I was watching the news on the big tv suspended on the wall beside us.

The volume wasn't on, so I had to read the subtitles which always annoys me as they never give you a word for word play by of what's is actually being said, quite often skipping words and leaving blanks to be filled in like a guessing game of what's happening.

After what seemed like a lifetime I was finally called into the department where I was to be assessed. I can't remember the doctors name although he was a lovely man who was very patient and thorough. He did every check he could think of and finally told me what I was dreading to hear, yes he also thought that I had bell palsy, quite severe, no they don't know what causes it or why it affects the face the way it does but predominately stress is a huge factor, but I wasn't to worry I was being given the strongest viral medication to take as I was still within the time frame, albeit barely, and this was the part I held on to with dear life, it wouldn't get any worse. In fact, I should be back to normal within two weeks by which point I will have a follow up appointment with a consultant doctor over at the Ear Nose and Throat clinic. Two weeks! I could handle that.

So off we went, medication in hand and some surgical tape to help keep my eye closed during the night as it wasn't blinking as it should, which meant it would dry out during the day. As we left, I was feeling a little better about the whole situation, I wasn't jumping for joy at being told that I had facial paralysis, but the doctor said it would only be around two weeks and that I was at the worst of it. I allowed myself that bit of relief, even if it was only minuscule. We drove back to mums for a coffee and had some lunch, in my case something that I could pull apart and place in my mouth as I struggled to eat on any side but the right. Biting into food such as sandwiches was no longer possible.

I took my medication regularly for the next two weeks, trying to avoid getting anxious about the lack of significant improvement.

I left the house only to drop off the kids and then I went straight back home again, hiding behind the safety of my front door. By the time my two-week appointment had arrived I was a physical and emotional wreck. My face had got increasingly worse, I could no longer drink from a cup and had to use a straw on the right-hand side of my mouth to drink anything at all, which by this point was mainly water as all the taste buds on the left-hand side were also completely gone, left behind was a bland rubber taste on one half of my mouth. Eating was already an issue but on top of having to only eat food I could place in my mouth in small pieces, now I had to be careful not to chew the inside of my left cheek as it was constantly getting caught within my teeth as I chewed. It was the weirdest thing, if I chewed a piece of gum on the right side of my mouth it was all minty fresh, as soon as I manoeuvred it over to the left it was like chewing a bland piece of rubber. It was entirely tasteless.

I hadn't gone back to work after all of this had started; I was far too self-conscious and embarrassed, plus I could not handle any high pitch noises at all, as you can imagine working in a school playground is full of happy kids shouting and squealing at the top of their lungs so that was out of the question, not that I would have gone in with a paralysed face anyway, and like I mentioned before my confidence was literally dragging behind me on the floor by this point, so after the original appointment at the hospital I had signed myself off for the foreseeable, which wasn't looking just like two weeks. The head at my school was really understanding, she had had a friend go through the same thing and didn't put any pressure on me to rush back to work. Just the sound of stirring a teaspoon around in a cup of coffee would hurt my ear, it was like all the very low sounds were fine, but any kind of high pitch noise just hurt to where I constantly was left covering my left ear until I could get hold of some cotton wool to stuff in there to block out the noise, it was the strangest sensation. Imagine having a horn held right next to your ear and then being blasted in short bursts, that was what it felt like, it literally hurt that much that I would have to hold my head to one side.

This ear sensation also involved other aspects. I could not submerge my head under water, in the bath I would have to hover my head just under the surface enough and tip my head back tolerating a neck ache so I could rinse the shampoo out of my hair otherwise if I held my head underneath the water, gradually a dull ache would begin deep inside my ear and it would linger for at least half an hour afterwards. Showers were trickier, any water that ran inside my ear would immediately cause the same ache which again lasted long enough for me to not bother with them anymore and just stuck with the baths as it was almost impossible to avoid the water running down into my ear.

A few weeks prior to all of this happening myself and my husband were meant to be taking the kids on their first all-inclusive abroad holiday to Cape Verde for our annual holiday. It was the first all-inclusive abroad holiday on a plane that we were taking the kids on and every one of us was super excited. Hot sandy beaches, whale watching and baby sea turtles laying eggs at midnight were all on the agenda, but what I hadn't told them was what if I couldn't fly? I couldn't handle any pressure under water so I was getting increasingly concerned that being in an airplane with cabin pressure might cause the same issue. The problem with my ear dragged on for months after and as it turned out, I needn't have worried anyway, covid put a stop to that trip.

Like the A&E doctor had predicted, my eyelid wasn't closing or blinking correctly so every night I had to tape my eye shut. This comprised of tearing off four even strips of medical tape and applying them over my eye in the shape of a plus symbol. Every morning, I would wake up dreading that when I slowly peeled off the tape, my lashes would all be removed with it, stuck to the tape glue. You would think being at home surrounded by your family that love and care for you unconditionally, you wouldn't really care how you look, but I did. I felt embarrassed in the mornings if anyone would wake up before me and come in to see the tape plastered over one eye, I even hid it under an eye mask, so it wasn't so apparent. No one needed to see me first thing in the morning with one eye taped closed looking like a deformed pirate, I certainly didn't like looking at it myself so I would try to spare the others. My husband and kids said and did all the right things to try and make me feel better.

The kids were heartbreakingly beautiful, telling me 'It wasn't that bad' and 'come on mum, smile it will get better, your smile is still beautiful' but every time I wanted to smile as I kissed them goodnight or talk to them about something that on any other time would have made me laugh or smile, I instantly felt like some kind of hideous gargoyle and tried my hardest to shy away without them realising.

God, I loved them for trying but the more they tried the more I wanted to just crumple and sob. I would regularly find myself behind the closed door to my bathroom, repeatedly punishing and tormenting myself by standing in the mirror and attempting to smile, to get some kind of movement, any movement at all, just so I didn't look like a distorted version of two face from the Batman movies, but it was no use. My face wouldn't move and every single time I would end up silently crying in the mirror at myself because of how ugly I felt I looked, which in turn would only make me cry harder as the more my face twisted and contorted through the sadness, the worse I felt I looked. I couldn't win either way. On the inside I was in a pretty dark place trying my best to act like it wasn't that bad and desperately trying to convince myself that it was only temporary, for the kids' sake as well as my own, but who was I kidding, it wasn't improving at all. In fact, it was only getting worse.

The Sadder Side of Me

Four

By the time I had reached the two weeks mark I couldn't even talk without having to hold the side of my mouth up. I thought drinking through a straw and eating little pieces of food were degrading enough but this was something else entirely. Just to hold a simple conversation or to even just give someone a one worded answer back required me to hold my left cheek and pull it up and to the side, just so I could speak clearly enough for them to understand me.

If I didn't, or if I forgot myself my words were slurred, and it felt really horrible. It had got to the point where I was now literally not going anywhere apart from dropping the kids off at school, keeping my head down avoiding any potential friends who may want to talk to me and getting home again. I would spend my days binge watching Netflix series or attempting to read my books. I now no longer could sit for hours immersed in a book. Anything longer than a few chapters would cause my eye to feel excessively dry and a headache would begin to burn at my temples.

To begin with I only allowed my mum and dad, my sister, brother and their families to come around, and that was only because they refused to allow me to wallow at home alone. A few days in on a visit to my parents' house I remember sitting in the lounge talking to my sister and my mum about something or another when my nephew, completely innocently looked directly at me and asked me what was wrong with my face and why was it doing that. For a split second I froze not knowing how to respond in an unemotional way but mainly focused on making sure that my face, the side that was working anyway, didn't relay the utter shock that was reverberating through me on the inside.

Obviously, everyone could see what was wrong and they all knew about my condition, but it wasn't really spoken about as they all knew I didn't like to highlight it, but kids are very simple beings, the world can quite simply on occasion be just black and white and they don't see the problem with pointing things out or asking questions about things that appear different. They are not afraid to ask why as they are just genuinely curious. It wasn't a question that was unreasonable, and he was only a kid so the usual etiquette that came with having a filter as an adult and not asking the obvious questions that might upset or offend are lost on most children, and especially my nephew, who I loved to pieces but who would regularly make me laugh with tales of his general lack of filter. I remember one such time my sister had regaled us of a trip they had out to grab a couple of bits for dinner at the local supermarket, both standing in line waiting to pay, when my nephew had said quite matter of factly and loud enough for most to hear,

'Eh what on earth is that smell' whilst promptly grabbing his nose.

'That's some serious BO, that man needs a shower' whilst scrunching his face up in disgust. At the time I could imagine my sister just desperately wishing the ground would swallow her whole but at the same time also trying really hard to not laugh at the look on her sons face whilst placating him and telling him to keep his voice down.

He didn't say these things out loud out of any malice, he just wasn't born with much of a filter and just says what is on his mind, which is just one of the reasons which makes him who he is, and I love him for that brutal honesty and curiosity in life.

So anyway, I went to explain as best as I could whilst trying to repeat over and over in my head 'don't get upset, don't get upset' but thankfully my sister stepped in and explained what had happened and why only the right side of my face was working, which he accepted with mild curiosity and moved on to the next thing that caught his attention. Gone within a fleeting moment, he got an answer and was happy enough to go off to play, totally consumed by other things. I sat there utterly trapped within my own head. I didn't want to cause a scene, and any amount of sympathy would have dislodged my fake carefree bravado that I was desperately holding in place. I left it as long as I could, which was probably only a few minutes even though it felt like a lot more, then I got up, pretended I needed a wee and sat in the toilet silently crying for as long as I thought I could get away with. This was where I was at. Any curiosity, any kind words or support given would send me on a downward spiral of gut-wrenching sadness for which all I wanted to then do was curl up in my bed and hide from the world. I just could not cope with what was happening and hated that it was so blaringly obvious to everyone.

One escape I always had when I needed a break was to read. I am a huge reader, I have a blog and social pages that I regularly post on, and I review books for publishers and authors on a regular basis, so to say reading was my passion would be quite the understatement. I get it from my dad, growing up I would always have a book on the go, as a child I took great pride in my bookshelves that were alphabetically stored in my room and even wrote a book when I was younger, writing out by hand the story and drawing and colouring in all the fruit characters. Even now whenever myself and my dad get together we could quite literally talk about what books we have read or plan to read for an immeasurable amount of time, much to my mums irritation of having to sit there and listen to the both of us waffle on when it is just the three of us in a room, she never has been a big reader, mostly only reading autobiography's, the complete opposite to the two of us who loved a good fictional story.

Even when the kids were younger, and I had at one point four kids under five years old running around keeping me busy, I would still manage to sneak in a bit of reading anywhere I could, but now I was finding that I could only read a page or two before I would have to stop. I was getting headaches, and the words would blur on the page causing my eyes to also ache. This was the last straw for me. It might not seem much to others, but reading was a way of getting out of my own head for a while, a way to de stress from having a busy household and being able to lose myself entirely in another time and place was a gift I enjoyed on a regular basis. I was heartbroken. I refused to stop reading though and would just pick up my book whenever I could and put it down whenever the headaches would inevitably start to kick in or when my eye started to feel overly dry, inwardly refusing to give in to the pain that was inevitable whenever I read.

By this point I had made it to the end of the two weeks marker that was meant to be the turning point for getting better, yet it was the worst it could have been.

Five

One afternoon, whilst visiting at my parents' house, my brother mentioned a friend he once knew from school who had tried acupuncture for bell's palsy and that she had had significant results from it. I was sceptical at first but after much googling I discovered that acupuncture was maybe an option that could possibly help alongside facial massages, so when my appointment came around with the consultant in the ENT department, I took my mum along with me as Justin was needed at work and I went with an open mind that I would ask for his advice on alternative treatments as the viral medication had seemingly done nothing to stop or slow down the disorders effects. This, I was about to find out was a needless task.

We arrived in the waiting room early and sat, anxiously waiting for my name to be called. There were only a few other people waiting, all of us trying to make the most of the uncomfortable plastic chairs that were lightly stuffed with minimal padding. There was no tv this time, so I flicked through a couple of the outdated magazines that were scattered along the edges to pass the time whilst I waited. After a short while I was called into the examination room and was met by a young doctor and his two female assistants. My mum came in with me for moral support and took a seat in the corner whilst I took a seat in the only other available chair that was positioned in the centre of the room.

I'll be honest here. This was about to become the worst moment of my life so far. -

The doctor was quite young and began to curtly ask me a few questions. He examined my face and then went on to tell me that my face probably wouldn't get better at all, in fact, and these were his words, IF it does improve then to expect it not to improve very much at all and that I would be left with a significant change. As you can imagine this was the last thing I wanted to hear, my world was quite literally falling apart around me as he spoke his uncaring and chipped words at me. Not once talking to me like a person who clearly had distress written all over their face, but at me like another task that needed to be completed before moving on to the next inconvenience. Refusing to allow my tears to fall in this cold ungiving room in front of this unkind and abrupt doctor, I took a breath, steadied myself and tentatively voiced my concerns about taping my eye shut. My question was would I have to keep using the tape as I was concerned it would pull out my eyelashes.

Obviously in the grand scheme of things my eye lashes are the least of my worries, BUT when you have half a face that is totally paralysed you try to salvage as much prettiness and normality as you can, and I know that sounds shallow but like I said before, I am not a confident person and always extremely conscious of how I look (I've recently found out from a therapist, that needing to look perfect and have control is an after effect of being bullied repeatedly in school.)

As I asked this question I was internally grasping at straws, trying to hold on to something positive, but no! He turned to me and in a very unsympathetic tone said "what is more important? Your eyelashes or your eyesight? Because if you continue to not tape up your eye properly then your eye will dry out and you will eventually become blind in that eye".

In that moment all I really needed was for a kind and understanding doctor to tell me what my options would be and that it wasn't necessarily permanent. I knew I wasn't going to walk in there and be told that it was going to be a quick fix and I also knew they couldn't tell me it would definitely go away, no matter how much I wanted to hear those words. I understood that wasn't a possibility, but to just have that caring and calm interaction would have made my experience so much better and easier to swallow, emotionally.

This was the point where I must have looked like a tiny, frightened animal. I sat in that chair in the middle of the room desperately trying to hold it all together. I couldn't really ask anything else because I was too busy desperately trying to control the lump in my throat that was so large it was tinkering on the edge of overflowing; I swallowed down the sobs that wanted to break free. The two lovely nurses honestly didn't know where to look, one turned around and gave me some tape and a pack of eyedrops to take home and the other offered me an apologetic smile. I then very stupidly mustered up the courage and asked this doctor who could not spare me an ounce of pity if it would be worth trying acupuncture as I had read that there was a chance it could possibly help. His reply was to the point and quite simply that he won't comment on that as it's an alternative form of medicine, there isn't any actual scientific evidence to back up that it works, and he doesn't hold much sway with its affects.

His parting words were "if you have any issues then give us a call, if not then we won't need to see you again". Basically, go home, put up and shut up. How could I be expected to just go home and get on with it? At this point I would like to just say that I don't doubt for one moment the NHS is stretched to its limits, this was before Covid was even a thing, but there was absolutely no need for that doctor to be so dismissive of me and my feelings. He was cold and callous to me as a patient. I'd like to think that he was most probably run off of his feet with work and being young was struggling to deal with the work load that I don't doubt was put upon him, but the other side of me argues that he is a doctor, he chose that profession and it isn't a secret that doctors need to be compassionate with patients and be aware of how that patient is taking the extremely damaging information that could affect their mental health.

I honestly believe that if I didn't have the support of my family and friends around me, and if I didn't know that there was an alternative therapy that could maybe help me, then my story would have been completely different. I know everyone has bad days, but when your bad day could tip the scales of someone else's, in a serious and damaging way then as a doctor compassion and mindfulness should always be paramount. I managed to get up, say a thank you to the nurses who both looked quite embarrassed by the doctor's attitude, and I walked out of that room, desperately trying to hold it all together. I couldn't look at my mum as I knew I would just crumble on the spot in an endless void of tears and not get back up again, so I kept my head down, as we walked around the corner and I excused myself into the nearest toilet I could find, which was thankfully just around the bend to where the waiting room was.

As soon as I shut the door I cried. Not gentle sad tears but tears that felt like they were going to consume me if I didn't get a hold of them. I cried as hard as I could but as silently as I could. I just needed to let all the emotion that had been slowly building like a clenched fist within the centre of my chest and throat the entire time I was in that room out. Then, after a few moments I pulled myself together, sorted myself out, pushed all that sadness way down deep and walked out to meet my mum.

Obviously, one look at me and she knew. But I wouldn't discuss it, couldn't if I wanted to make it to the carpark whilst keeping up appearances making my way through the hospital. I certainly could not cry in front of anyone, it looked too weird as only half my face showed expression. Even I didn't like to look at it. We went back to the car and on the way home I asked if it was ok to drop her off at home as I just needed to be by myself. That was her red flag. I never, ever ditched my mum. My family are my go-to whenever I'm sad or angry and usually I would go back to hers and we would talk it all out, I would have a little cry and then we would do something to take my mind off of it, usually cake or lunch. But this time I couldn't do it, I just needed to go home, climb under my duvet and hide from the world, to allow myself to fall headfirst into that black void I now felt myself slipping steadier and faster into.

Six

I dropped mum off and drove straight home a complete snivelling mess. I didn't hold back in the car. As soon as I was out of sight, I drove the entire way home ugly crying, loud and untamed. I walked straight through the front door, up the stairs and crawled into bed. That was where I stayed for the next hour. I cried and cried and cried. I literally have never cried so much in my life, proper chest heaving, uncontrollable intense and heart-breaking sobbing. I didn't care that my bedroom window was open, and my neighbour could possibly hear my cries. They were guttural and I buried my head into my pillow and just released it all. I gave in, allowed the wave of sadness to wash over me and accept that deep need to hide away from the entire world and withdraw from everything. All that strength and hope from the last few weeks had just been ripped away leaving me raw and open.

This is the point where my hubby showed me just how much he truly loved me. Obviously I knew he did, he was and always is affectionate, showing me in all the little ways that matter how much he loves me And it's in those little things, the things said or done that make you realise that this person, whom you promised to love in sickness and in health actually would love you totally and completely, not that I ever doubted him for a second but it was just what I needed in that moment of feeling so alone. My mum had given him a call shortly after I had dropped her off to let him know what had happened at the hospital, he had left work and came straight home. As soon as he opened the front door, he ran straight up the stairs and into our bedroom. He found me lying on the bed a complete mess. I managed to tell him through broken sobs the short version of what the doctor had said, to which I followed up with how he could want to stay with me, I can never smile again, never go out on a date again and never kiss him properly again.

It may seem like an inconsequential thing but in my eyes, kissing can be a more intimate act than that of sex. It pulls you closer and forces you to truly look at the person in front of you, to show the person that is before you that you love them most in the world. It's a tenderness that is exclusive between just the two of you, a bonding force that reconnects you both after a row, a sign of your love before going to sleep and a way to say goodbye for the day without the need for words. In that moment I genuinely couldn't imagine ever being able to kiss my husband on the mouth ever again, kiss my children goodnight or even to simply blow them a kiss, a silent display that says unequivocally, I love you, and it broke my heart even further. He simply shuffled over to me, pulled me into his side, hugged me tight and told me that he loved me no matter what I looked like. He didn't marry me for my face and that we would find a way together. I loved him so much in that moment, despite my emotional state I could see how concerned he was for me.

I attempted to lighten the mood for him, to make him smile and I guess to distract myself a little, I stated our usual running joke about his hair (that we don't mention is ever so slightly thinning the older he gets) I said that he had well and truly got me over a barrel now because how could I ever leave him when he finally goes bald if he is perfectly happy to have me looking the way I do, but it didn't work, his answer was quite simply 'well your stuck with me now, no getting out of this one girlie' I could see written all over his face and in his eyes that he was trying so hard to make me feel better, but it didn't quieten the devil that was sitting in my ear, telling me how hideous I looked.

Everything spiralled from there. In my eyes there would be no more going out with other couples for dinner, I would only be the weird one struggling to eat out of one side of her mouth and sipping drink through a straw anyway, I could rule nights out with the girls, drinking and having a laugh. Even the simplest things in life like enjoying a hot cup of black coffee from my favourite tall mug my best friend brought me for my birthday that I only used in the mornings when I had my first cup of the day because it held the most caffeine would no longer be a simple pleasure.

It hit me with pure unfiltered clarity just how I had taken all the little things in life for granted, not ever considering that they could all be taken away in a split second overnight. I'd never look anyone in the eye again confidently and have a conversation. My life would quite simply be reduced to hiding inside my house, avoiding eye contact at every opportunity, and limiting as much as possible the amount of people I have face to face contact with. As for photos, that wasn't ever happening again. I couldn't bear to look at my face and I certainly wasn't about to be reminded in years to come what I looked like as I was pretty sure it would get worse with age. I hated how I looked, and I knew deep down that I was not a strong enough person to live the rest of my life with what I felt was only half a face.

Despite this harrowing feeling, having children was paramount to me and I would never consider anything that would take me away from them, they are more important to me then my own life and I would never do that to them but, and this is a huge but, I could feel I was tapping ever so slightly on depressions door, and I knew that it was just an inevitable downward slope for me to slowly sink into. Always to play the part of being happy on the outside but on the inside, I would forever feel alone, sat curled at the bottom of a very dark and lonely cave, only looking up to see the light at the end of a tunnel, a happiness, and a carefree contentment always fully just out of my reach. It sounds dramatic but, in my head, at that time that's the only way to describe how I felt, every minute of every day.

It was an odd Christmas that year. Usually, my whole family would gather and meet up at my parents'

house to sit around the tree and open gifts from
each other after dinner. It was a yearly tradition we
all enjoyed gathering around to enjoy the evening
drinking, eating copious amounts of snacks and
talking whilst a Christmas movie played in the
background and the kids were all off amusing
themselves with their latest gadgets and toys, but for
me I was only a month in of having only half a face so
the thought of going round and eating at my parents'
house filled me with dread. They completely
understood when I explained that I couldn't come,
they even tried to convince me that it may be better to
go as I would be distracted enough to maybe forget
about it for a while, but I knew this wasn't me and
there was no way I could sit around everyone whilst
they chatted and laughed knowing every response
albeit laughter or talking would be hidden behind my
hand. Even sitting at my own dinner table with the
kids and Justin was going to be hard work, every
piece of food I tried to eat would have to be cut up
small and placed into the right side of my mouth and I
could feel my left not responding as I chewed on the
opposite side as the left hadn't improved at all and
was still just like eating rubber and only led to me
biting my cheek, so I covered my mouth again with
every bite. I hated every minute of it all. Really, I
wanted to bury my head in the sand and cancel
Christmas just so there was no expectation to look

happy, so the kids wouldn't feel the constant need to check that I was ok, so I could just have a neutral expression on my face and not feel like I felt like an ugly deformed woman. Obviously, I would never have done that, the kids always came first but that's how I genuinely spent my Christmas.

Christmas that year you wouldn't find me in a single photo.

Seven

This next part is a bit of a blur for me, if I'm honest I was too sad, to broken and just to mentally exhausted to remember everything like I did in the beginning, but what I do remember is how my husband and children emotionally tried really hard to support me whilst my family went out of their way to look up the alternative therapy that could possibly help me. My brother told me again one afternoon about that friend he knew from school who had recently suffered from Bell's Palsy, she had used acupuncture therapy, and it was a success. I am not a fan of needles so the thought of having lots of them stuck into my face wasn't a very appealing prospect, but he also suggested mum came along with me and we have it done together. Mum suffers from awful migraines so she could get treated for those whilst I was treated for my facial palsy. At this point I was out of options and said I would be willing to give anything a try, if she would. Luckily for me my sister told me she knew about an acupuncture clinic about twenty minutes away from where we lived where a colleague of hers had used and found really helpful. I knew if I delayed it any further, I would chicken out, so I grabbed my phone, looked up the number and gave them a call. The lady on the other end of the line was very sweet, she had quite a strong Chinese accent but was clear enough and she politely booked me in for the following Friday at ten am.

It wasn't a long drive; the town wasn't that far, and the journey was quite pleasant as most of it runs alongside the sea. After driving completely past the shop and parking in the wrong spot at the totally wrong end of the street, we walked all the way back up the long road in the rain and finally saw the little shop front that was used as a clinic on the corner of the road. The clinic was a tiny little building run by an older Chinese couple, who came across as very open and friendly. As we walked through the door the waiting room was big enough for maybe four or five people at a push, the desk was a bit like a vintage style teacher desk set in the corner as the front of the clinic was almost hexagonal in shape. The wall directly in front of you as you walk in was full up with what I can only describe as the old-fashioned sweet containers, full to the brim of Chinese herbal remedies, this ran all the way around to the side of the shop front covering half of the window. I loved it; I was totally in awe of all the different concoctions that were being held within those plastic jars. They looked like the type of herbal medicines that would have been used for centuries, promising an ancient cure better than any modern medicine.

I gave the lady my name and turned to take a seat in one of the two chairs that were lining the window behind me. Before we had even sat down my acupuncture doctor, an Older Chinese man with a very open and friendly face smiled and called us through. I couldn't help but notice he had a slight facial paralysis too, but I wasn't confident enough to ask and felt it may come across as rude.

We followed him down a slim passage and into the first consultation room on the left. The room was small and narrowish, long enough for a bed and chair at the foot of it and wide enough to comfortably fit a desk and chair. I sat down on the bed whilst my mum took a seat at the foot of the bed. The doctor stood before me, introduced himself as Dr Li and kindly asked what he could do to help. He also had quite a strong accent like the lady at the front desk, his smile and friendly manner were very relaxing even though I was anxious that I was about to sign myself up to willingly having numerous amounts of needles stuck into my body; I cannot even look when a blood sample is being taken, so you can guess where my anxiety levels were at!

I explained about my face as best as I could and after he asked me a few questions about how it all started and where exactly the numbness began, he confidently told me that he could treat me with acupuncture and that he was also confident that he could make me better and get my face back to normal again (that's my interpretation of what he said in a nutshell, his choice of words were much more professional) I literally felt like a weight had shifted ever so slightly from my shoulders, having gone from being told there was nothing that could be done to being shown a light at the end of a very dark tunnel and at a price that wasn't overly expensive. I put all my fears aside and took a chance. I was then caught off guard when Dr Li offered to start my treatment there and then, I wasn't expecting this, I assumed it would just be a consultation to begin with and I was not prepared to have anything done in that moment, that was something I would need to work up to, I knew it was cowardly but I made my excuses despite the side look I was getting from my mum and we booked an appointment for the following Friday to begin our treatment. I needed at least a week to mentally prepare for this one.

The week flew by, and it wasn't long before we were back sitting in the waiting room anxiously awaiting our first treatment. Like before, we were called through pretty quick, I was guided into the first room I was put in from my original consultation and my mum was sent to the second room next door, followed by Dr Li.

After a few minutes Dr Li came back and asked me to remove my socks and shoes and to lie on my right-hand side. He then proceeded to take out of the packets of needles that he was going to use.

He explained that it shouldn't hurt and to just relax. This was obviously easier said than done On the outside I was attempting to remain calm and composed but, on the inside, I was absolutely terrified, the only sign you would have noticed that I was full of fear was from my hand, it was clenched tight, I can imagine my fingers must have looked a shade of white from the intensity of the squeeze, also my jaw was firmly set. He noticed this though despite my best efforts, he gently unclenched my hand, smiled, and assured me everything was fine and again to just try and relax.

Eight

As he began his examination of where to place the needles, I could feel him feeling his way around my face, his fingertips searching for specific nerve areas gently so that he could clearly feel from years of training that was not visible to the naked eye. I can't honestly say that when the needles went in, they hurt but I did feel it. The sensation was instantly sharp (again not a painful sharp) followed by a split second of pressure, not pain exactly but an awareness that it had gone through the skin. The needles were always positioned on the left side of my face.

To start with I had nine needles in total situated in my head, two went into my hand and finally four in my feet. Of the nine that were in my head, three were in my cheek nerves, two of which were placed along the line that runs from the outside of my left nostril to the corner of the mouth, another was placed in the centre of my cheek just under the cheek bone (this was and still is my worst nerve) three were placed in my forehead; one just above the outside arch of my eyebrow, with another positioned a few centimetres above the centre of the same arch, and the third went into my forehead along my hairline.

One went just inside my ear within the fold above the ear canal, another just below the lobe in the crevice at the base of my ear and lastly one was placed within the back of my neck just behind my ear. Like I said, they didn't always hurt going in as they went in so quick, but they did feel uncomfortable for a few seconds after they sank into the nerves. As for my hand, I had one placed an inch above the centre of my wrist on my forearm and another in the soft fleshy part of my hand in-between the thumb and forefinger. Out of all the needles stuck in my nerves this one was the hardest to cope with. Every session lasted around thirty minutes and for the entire time I was there, it took all my will power not to move any of my fingers on that hand. I'm not sure if you're like me at all but I have always been the kind of kid growing up that if I was told not to touch something, it would then be like a bright neon arrow pointing to whichever it was I was warned not to put my hands on. I would have the biggest of urges to touch that exact thing and it would be like my fingers were restless, itching to reach out and touch the forbidden. It never really went away as an adult either, if I had a sore tooth, I would clench my teeth just to feel if the pain was still there even though it would ache every time I did it. The same was with my hand.

Every time I moved a finger, even the slightest twitch and the nerve in the soft fleshy part would twang and send an uncomfortable electrifying sensation that would shoot right through my hand and wrist. You know the feeling you get when you bang your elbow on a doorframe and your so-called funny bone gives you a rather unfunny sensation like you have just had the nerve plucked like a violin string, well that was what it was like, and it drove me mad every single week. Having to fight that compulsive need to twitch a finger, knowing if I did, I would hate the electrical shock my raw nerve would give me in return was pure mental torture. Finally, the last needles were within the feet. Three in my left foot, all placed in the soft spaces below the central toes in-between the bones and one in my right foot again in the same area but in line with my little toe.

When he had completed making a pin cushion out of me Dr Li then covered my ear with a blue pad, quite similar to a squishy cardboard square and then proceeded to pull over an old looking lamp, a little like a desk lamp that is similar to the bouncing lamp from the beginning of the Pixar movies, except this one was old and faded. It was positioned above my ear, close enough for me to feel the heat quite intensely. This, he said was to stimulate the blood flow whilst the needles were allowing my nerves to be open.

This lamp constantly made me nervous and on edge. On more than one occasion I was convinced it had spat a tiny ember of heat onto my face making me physically recoil. It was quite close and looked like it had been around for a while, considering I had to spend the next half an hour not moving, just staring around the room I imagined quite a few times that heat lamp slipping on its stand and landing my face, then I would spiral off with the thoughts of how long it would take me to get up and get it off before it sizzled my skin. Not as easy a task as you would think as remember I was lying on my right hand side, my right arm tucked underneath me and I had many nerves being held in place by super fine needles, so much so that the slightest move would send electric shocks fizzing down the entire length of my body, so it would not have been a pleasant or easy task to complete.

My imagination used to run wild, placing myself in all kinds of scenarios from a fire slowly breaking out somewhere in the clinic to having my face burnt to a crisp by the antique lamp that had seen better days. All crazy situations would run through my mind to see if I could mentally work out a way that I could physically escape, whilst getting around the fact that I was technically pinned to the bed, all in a bid to keep myself entertained.

It's amazing what the brain can come up with if forced to do nothing but think. Thankfully I never needed to escape from my position on the bed. I did however hear my mum on the other side of the wall having her first treatment for her migraines. This also gave me plenty to think about as I didn't have a clue what she was having done, I could just hear the doctor talking her through her positioning. Every six- or seven-minutes Dr Li came back into the room to ask if I was ok and to move the heat lamp alternatively between my face, hand, and feet.

Finally, my half hour was up, and the ancient lamp was turned off and twisted away, the metal legs squeaking in protest. One by one the needles were removed, again an uncomfortable feeling was left in their wake for a few seconds of them being unpinned from my nerves until finally all of them were out. Quite surprisingly the doctor then came over and did a firm dance with his fingertips across my forehead. Imagine yourself tapping your fingers on the table starting with your pointer finger and then in turn ending with your pinkie, a drumming in sequence motion.

This is how it felt from across the centre of my forehead to my temple. Then he firmly pressed on the area beneath my cheek bone, gently applying pressure on and off for a few seconds at a time. This was, and still is my most sensitive area on that side of my face, it's like out of all the nerves that fan across from my ear just under the skin, this one is the most inflamed, the angriest, and the main one that always lets me know on a regular basis that it's still there, just beneath the surface, waiting to remind me.

Before I left that day, he strictly told me that I needed to massage my face every day in circular motions to keep stimulating the blood flow through the nerves, otherwise they would most likely stay in their paralysed state and never return to full function. I hopped off the bed, put on my socks and shoes, thanked him, and went out to the reception to pay and rebook for the following week. My mum was already waiting for me when I came out, expectantly searching my face to see how it went, I smiled as best as best as I could, pushing down the feelings of despair at not feeling any immediate improvements with my false hope. In my mind I replayed the mantra; I was fine, it'll all be ok, and we both left. This time the car was parked just around the back in the one parking space dedicated to the acupuncture centre. It was literally a one car space that was gravelled with a shed to the very back, parking in it was a little tricky and a big squeeze but it was a much better alternative to finding a space to park on the busy road.

As we drove to the shops nearby to pick up something for lunch, we chatted about how it all went, mum felt her treatment went well but hadn't eased any of her symptoms from the migraines so far. I, on the other hand was beginning to feel something I hadn't felt in the last few weeks, something I wasn't prepared to feel so soon. Despite all of my reservations and devil whispering on my shoulder moments. Hope was beginning to bud deep down in my stomach, and it terrified me.

The Sadder Side of Me

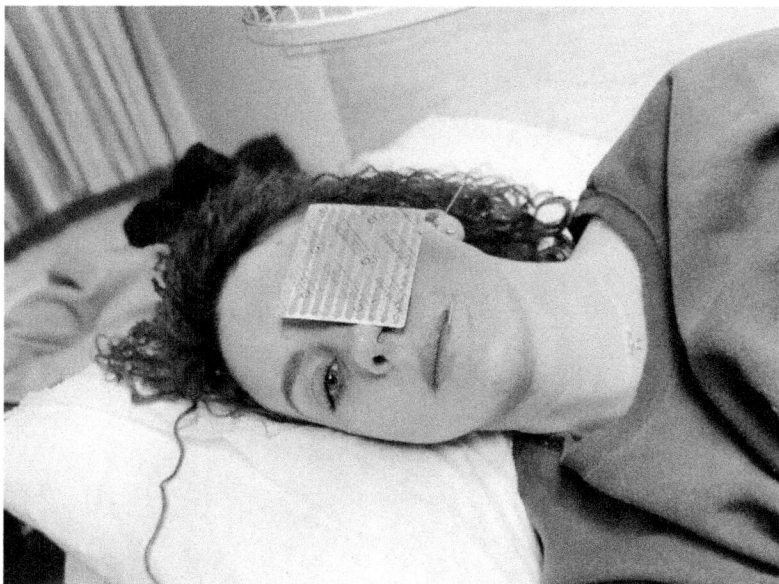

Claire Rowden

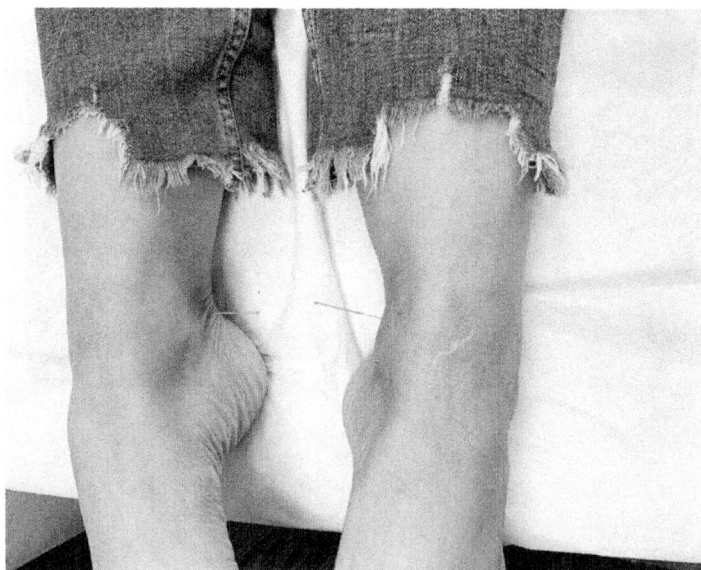

The Sadder Side of Me

Claire Rowden

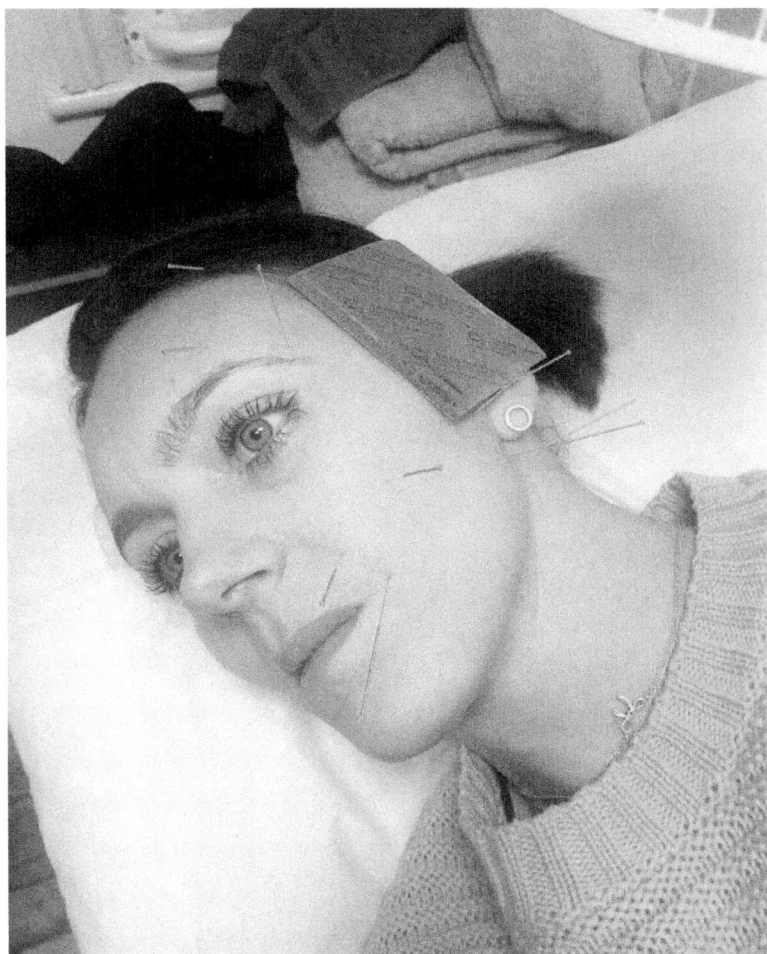

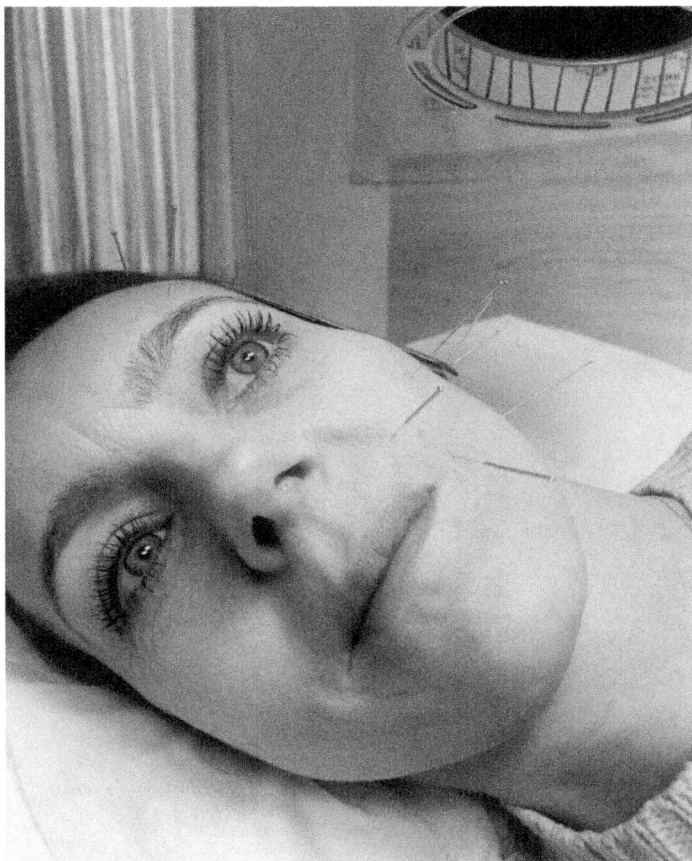

Claire Rowden

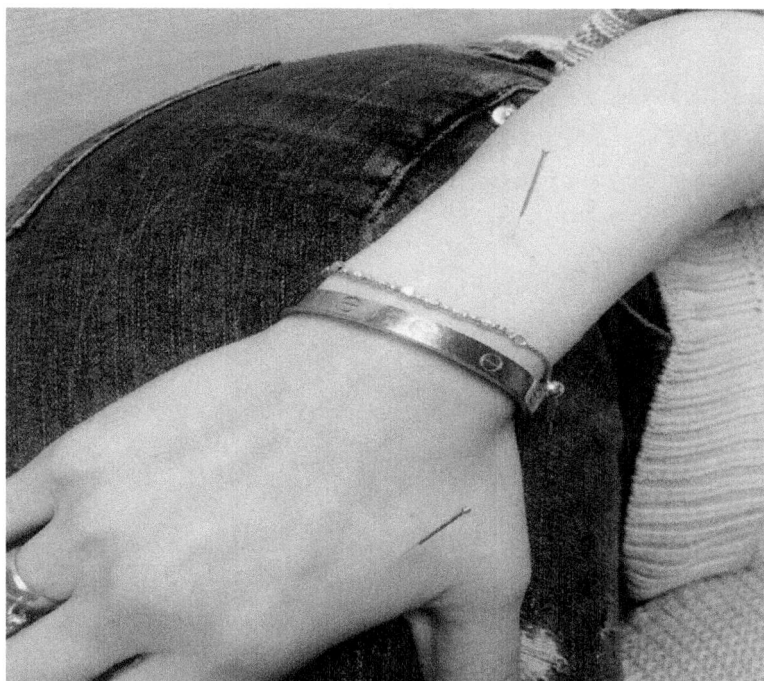

The Sadder Side of Me

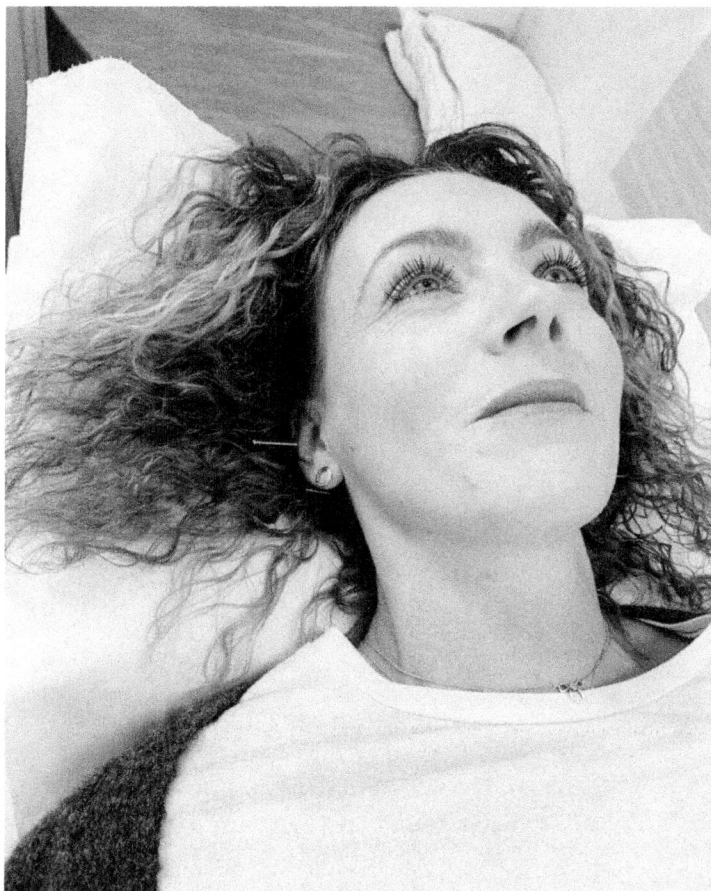

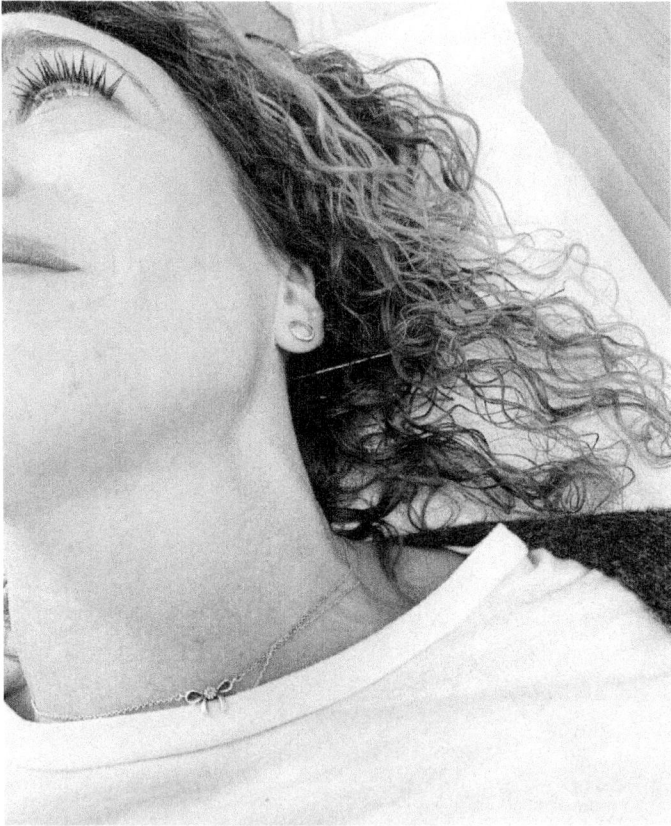

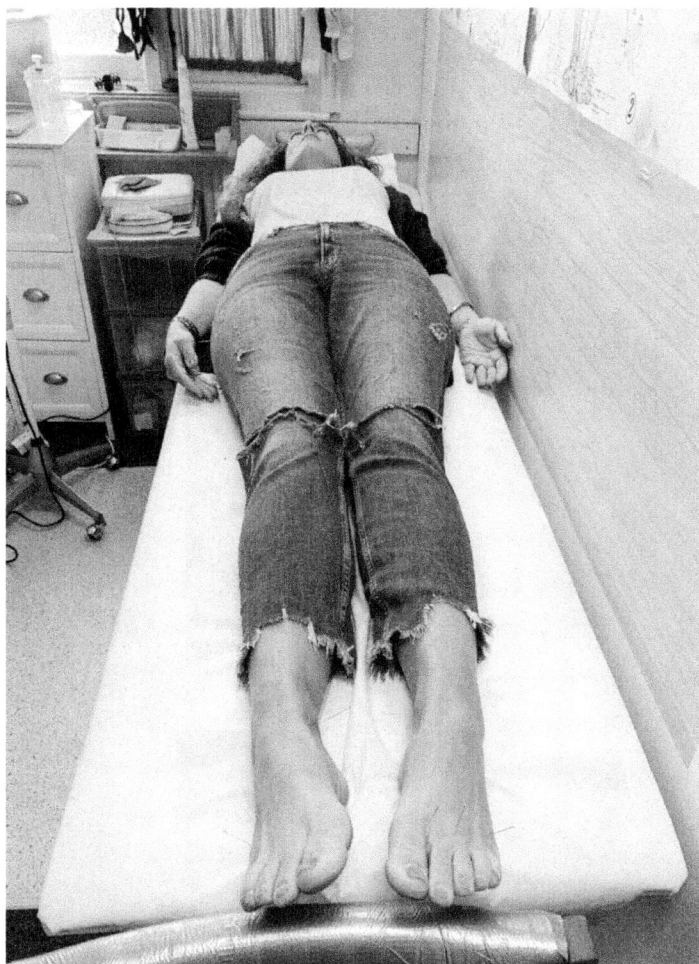

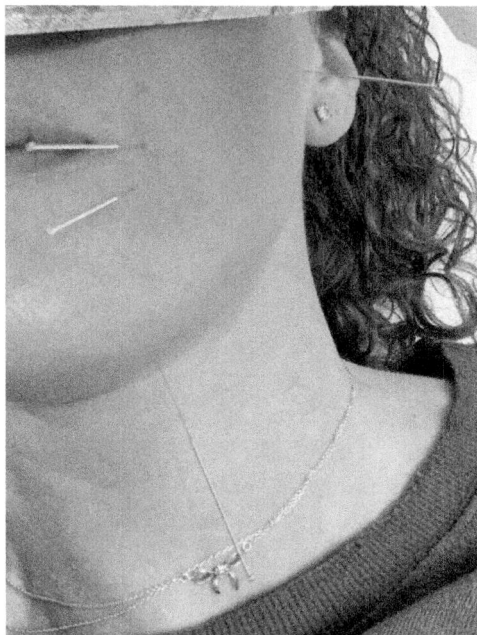

The Sadder Side of Me

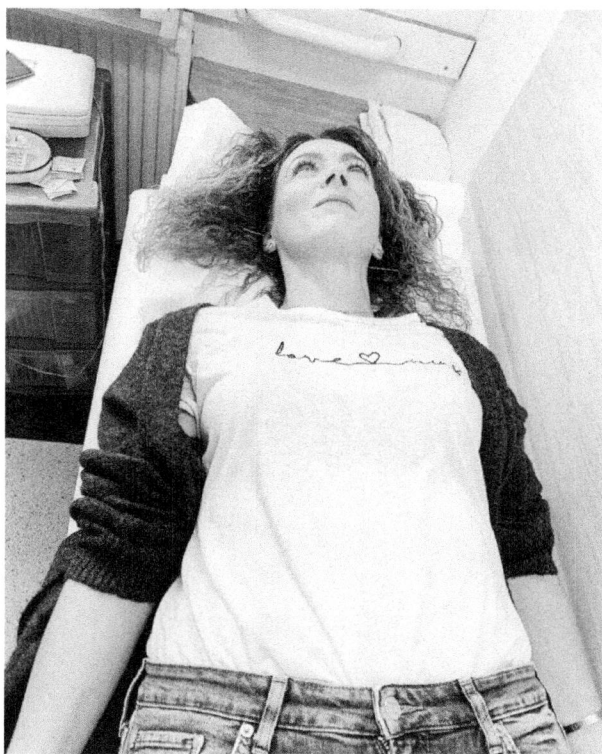

Claire Rowden

Nine

The rest of the day went by like normal and uneventful; well, the new normal for me, I picked up the big kids from senior school then drove back to the juniors to collect the younger two, keeping the lower half of my face hidden behind a scarf. Thankfully for me it was December, so it was cold enough to get away with it without drawing too much attention to myself. When I got home, I settled the kids with whatever they needed to keep them satisfied for the short amount of time that I needed to myself, and I slowly made my way up the stairs. I wanted to look in the mirror to see if I could notice any difference, even though I knew deep down that there was a high probability that there wouldn't be any as it was only my first session. To say my feet felt heavy and my heart felt weighted down with the dreaded anticipation would just about sum up how I was feeling walking up those stairs.

I sat on the edge of my bed and tentatively reached for the cosmetic mirror on my makeup desk and apprehensively inspected every inch my face. I sat there for a few moments trying to move my face in all different positions; from screwing up my nose, raising my eyebrows and trying to squeeze my eye shut, literally attempting everything and anything, silently willing there to be some kind of change. But I couldn't see anything. Just as I was beginning to let the disappointment take hold, which would inevitably be followed by the tears that I could feel building, knowing that they would not be falling gently I caught a glimpse of something out the corner of my eye, I noticed just the tiniest of movements. In a small area on my cheek, along the side of my nose I realised that if I scrunched up my nose enough a tiny patch of skin, no bigger than a five pence piece, moved. Actually, moved by itself!! This was huge! I could not believe that after just one session I had a bit of movement in my face. Ok so it was only a little patch of skin, but to me it meant that I had a chance to get my face back, it meant I no longer had to just hope that this might possibly work, and it was the sign I needed that told me all might not be lost. Obviously after spending far too long watching this miraculous little movement in the mirror, I then got out my phone and immediately began to record it, sending it to my family WhatsApp chat group to show them the result of my first session. I literally wanted to shout it to the world.

At this point I was over the moon. I had been through something that I was terrified of doing, it didn't necessarily hurt, and I walked away ache free. The elation I felt I could only assume was quite akin to just finding out that you had just won the lottery that you decided to take a one-off chance on, and I genuinely couldn't believe that it was going to be this easy.

This wasn't to be how I felt after every session unfortunately, but I never gave up regardless of how painful it got.

Ten

Every Friday morning at ten thirty I had my appointments booked in with Dr Li. Some sessions were easy, others not so much. The needles were always placed in roughly the same areas but there were a few occasions when, being a handful of treatments in, he would twist the needles once they were placed deep into my nerve which was not a pleasant sensation and a couple of times when we left if I opened my mouth, I would get a sharp shooting pain run down the length of my jaw. This was extremely uncomfortable, so I spent the rest of those days not really talking and opening my mouth as little as possible.

Other times I would leave thinking all was ok only to get the same shooting pain the second I tried to eat, it wasn't a short inconvenience either, again I would spend the entire day not being able to eat or drink anything for fear of getting that blinding pain radiate across my jaw. My nerves were obviously starting to slowly wake up and pay attention to what was being done to them and to be fair I had more sessions where I walked away relatively pain free than what I did in pain, and this gave me the courage I needed to continue with my treatment whenever I was too nervous to go back, anxiety rippled like a pool in the middle of my chest just in case I would have a dodgy session and I would suffer for the rest of the day.

During my weekly appointments I got to know every inch of that pale white, small rectangle room. A little window that looked out on to the side road sat high up at one end and above was scattered with square yellowing ceiling tiles. My mum had completed all of her sessions by this point and was enjoying the after effects of her treatment, although sometimes I really think coming to get an alternative treatment for her migraines was just an excuse she used to placate me as I don't think she genuinely wanted to get pricked with needles once a week but knew that I wouldn't have been so willing to give it a try if she hadn't agreed to have it done with me. Just another reason why my parents are the best in the world, always putting themselves up for things they wouldn't necessarily choose to do in order to make their children more comfortable.

So, I would lie there every week not able to really talk, if I did it would be out of the corner of my mouth, and mum would look up from her position in the chair at the foot of the bed, her phone in her hand and tell me to keep quiet and try to go to sleep. Like

that was ever going to happen with a face full of
needles and a heat lamp that occasionally spat
something at me! What it actually was I don't know,
but occasionally, I would feel a tiny, minuscule sting
of heat that clearly had to have come from the worn
lamp. Mum would entertain herself on her phone
whilst I did the only thing, I could do which was to
wait, to not move so I spent my sessions discovering
my surroundings.

The rectangle room had the bed positioned along the
wall on the right-hand side. Above it there were two
large posters detailing the human bodies, one female
and one male. Both naked with what looked like a
thousand lines pointing to every inch of the body, all
informing of what parts of the body were used to
place the needles in for what condition it could treat. I
found these fascinating, the needles could quite
literally be put everywhere – in and out of the human
body. On the left-hand side of the room sat the white
wooden desk which was littered with different boxes
of needle types in packets, antiseptic wipes and other
medical books and papers. A yellowing cast of a
spine and hip bones pinned in place on a block to be
inspected and turned around sat proudly to the side
and a landscape framed photo of a ceremony in China
hung above. There must have been about a hundred
men and women all standing on the steps of what I

assumed was a university posing for the photo with a banner proudly hung suspended above them in a language I couldn't read.

It reminded me of my senior school photo where the whole of year eleven were instructed to sit in the stands for that final picture before we all left school. I spent ages every week searching the sea of unknown faces on that image from across the room, desperately looking for Mr. Li, every time I thought I had located him I would be convinced it was someone else entirely. I couldn't physically get up and look closer and the thought had never occurred to me to take a closer look whenever my session was finished. The only other thing on that wall was a framed piece of white A4 paper. This is the piece of paper that I read and re read every single session without fail; the words on the page demanding my attention even though by the second session I knew every word. It was homemade, glued to the top was a photograph of Mr. Li holding a newborn baby in what appeared to be a dated hospital room. The handwritten message under neath was from a family thanking Mr. Li for everything he had done for them. Giving them hope after having had to endure years of failed IVF treatments. He had been their last chance at a shot at parenthood. The impression I got through this emotional piece of writing was that the doctor they had seen before had told them that the chances of them conceiving naturally were not good and with the IVF also failing, they were literally giving it one more try with something new. I could feel the emotion that was encapsulated within those few handwritten lines on a standard piece of plain a4 white paper. From having acupuncture, they had successfully fallen pregnant and had given birth to a healthy baby boy. The look of pride held with Dr Li's smile as he held the baby in his arms shone from the photograph.

I remember reading this beautiful message every single time I lie on that bed. Every single week I wondered how it could be possible that there are probably so many more people, like myself that had absolutely no clue just how powerful acupuncture could be and I could not help but think if only the NHS would recommend this form of treatment as an alternative, how many other people like myself and this young couple could have the happy ending they always thought was just outside of their reach. For some it could finally be an end to a crippling pain or a child they had desperately longed for but wasn't able to have. There were so many complaints that the human body could suffer from that painkillers just either didn't work on or their effect just diminished after a time of prolonged use. This thought regularly entered my mind as I lie there, and I could not help but think how arrogant the NHS were being. This alternative form of medicine has been around for centuries, long before medication was discovered, so I just could not wrap my head around the fact that it was discounted so easily by medical professionals.

Eleven

As well as having acupuncture once a week and sticking religiously to the rules of having to massage my face daily during my treatment period, I also had a weekly aromatherapy face massage which proved so beneficial for my nerves and my mental health combined. The lady who was my beautician, Vanessa, was a mum from the school that my younger children went to. She was Australian, absolutely beautiful (but the kind of person who didn't realise how pretty they actually were) and the nicest person I've ever met. Each Wednesday evening, I would go to her home, and we would go through to her beauty cabin at the end of her garden. Once inside you would not think that you were inside a small log cabin in the middle of a housing estate, it felt more like you was in a rural, welcoming spa with warm, ambient music, overhead lights that were dimmed down low and scented candles dotted along the side wall.

In amongst the peaceful serenity that comes with being totally relaxed on a spa bed, we would quite often chat about our daily lives whilst I was having my treatment. Vanessa would focus predominately on the left side of my face, and she would also know exactly where I needed the tension taking out of my neck and shoulders, which was a lot! It always took her quite a while to release some of the knots that had built up, but I always left feeling lighter and more relaxed and smelling heavenly. Going to those weekly sessions was the highlight of my week. It was an hour of my time where I could switch off my phone, totally relax and allow myself to be pampered. Leaving, my neck and shoulders always felt amazing from having the stress and tension of the week forced to leave my body and my face, even though physically it wouldn't show any signs of change, on the inside I would feel a hundred times better. When I would put the kids to bed on those facial nights, my youngest son would always smell my face as I gave him a kiss goodnight, always inhale deeply, and tell me how nice my face smelt.

As I said before, she was such a beautiful soul inside and out, if I saw her on the school run in the mornings, instead of hanging my head and hiding my face I force myself to be sociable, make eye contact and say hello, whilst at the same time attempting to hide as much as I could. In return she would always tell me how pretty or lovely I looked in the most natural and conversational way. It was such a lovely thing to say, and it always made me feel a little happier whenever I saw her, it gave my brain the much needed few moments of respite from constantly feeling like the ugliest mum on the school run.

Around the same time as my condition, my son was a goalie in a football team, and I used to have to take him every Sunday morning for goalie training. Being the middle of January it was absolutely freezing so I could get away with hiding behind my chunky knit scarf for the most part but on the odd occasion the coach would want to talk to me, I would have to try and discreetly hold my face up and to the side whilst talking to him so that he would have a shot at understanding the words I was trying to articulate back to him without slurring. I hated this; I was so embarrassed. As it was, I had to wear sunglasses because the wind would make my eye water, it would only be a slight breeze from standing in an open field, but my eye would react like a full-scale wind was blowing directly into it; not being able to blink as much would also cause my eye to dry out, which in turn would cause the excessive watering. It was so frustrating. These are the moments when I wished I could just stay at home and not face anyone. This didn't always go to plan though either. A friend came over one afternoon to see how I was, like I've mentioned previously, I try to put a brave face on my pain and pretend everything was ok but sitting in the lounge over coffee I made the mistake of telling her about a dream I had the previous night. In my dream I woke up, went to the bathroom like normal to brush my teeth, but this time when I looked up and glanced in the mirror, I noticed instantly that my face was completely back to normal, it was like the bells palsy had never even existed. I could smile, laugh, frown and blink to my heart's content. Then I woke up. Reality came charging down on me like a steam train at full speed. I turned over, pulled the duvet up around my shoulders and quietly sobbed, making sure to not wake up Justin who slept peacefully beside me as I just felt so silly. As I told her this the emotions unexpectedly slammed into me like a brick wall halfway through, totally catching me off guard as I thought I had a handle of myself and was doing well to keep it all together. It was such a heart-breaking dream that I ended up spontaneously crying for a moment, covering my face with my hands to hide my pain from my friend and the kids who had all stopped still, shocked at my sudden show of grief and usure how to react, but also to hide my distorted face.

I still hate that I did that in front of them, they were all there in the lounge doing one thing or another, kind of minding their own business as I caught up with my friend. The room fell instantly silent when I became upset, you could have heard a pin drop. They didn't know what to do, so they all paused and didn't move, not wanting to do or say the wrong thing. I sorted myself out quickly, I'm pretty good at that, pushing down my emotions and tucking them deep down to be dealt with at a later date. I told them I was fine and assumed they would accept that and move on. But I recently found out that afterwards, my little girl went upstairs and had a cry because she was so sad that I was so upset. It's hard trying to send out the messages to our children that we really need and want them to learn, whilst trying to master the art of showing them ourselves without losing control.

I know now that it is healthy for my children to see me cry, it shows them that its ok to be sad and have a cry if your upset about something. But I hate it. I hate them seeing me broken and vulnerable. And it breaks my heart that it makes them so sad. I'm the mum so in my eyes I should be strong at all times... that's how I felt but I also know that just teaches them to hide their emotions and I didn't want that. Just another reason why parenting is one of the hardest jobs physically and emotionally.

Twelve

I had a lot of time to reflect during those first few weeks as to why I might have been stressed out enough for my entire left side of my face to 'fall' as I had begun to call it. I'm usually a bit of a stress head, I have some control issues, and I worry a lot about things that don't always need worrying over; also, I had raised four children under five at one point pretty much single handed as Justin worked six days a week, sometimes seven if we needed, so being busy and on the go was kind of the norm for me. But thinking back it slowly started to become clear.

The previous year I had three big things happen all at the same time, all were very stressful and emotionally taxing. In the May I had a major operation on my ankle that I had been waiting for. For the two years previous I had spent them on and off with a medical boot on my right ankle to try and strengthen the tendons and ligaments. Over the years it had steadily gotten weaker to the point where it would roll and make me fall just walking on a flat surface with flat shoes on. So, a surgery that required opening up along the outside of my right ankle bone and cutting back the tendons and ligaments that had all stretched over the years due to repeated ankle rolling since I was a teenager was booked. The more it rolled the further stretched they became, and I guess at some point they lost the elasticity needed to hold me up. It wouldn't even support itself whilst lying on my back asleep in bed, I would quite often wake up from my foot falling abruptly to the side. It wasn't a great sensation.

Despite being in theatre, a lot longer than expected, the surgery actually went well. I had my right leg in a cast from toes to knee and was forbidden to put any weight whatsoever on my foot for twelve weeks, plus it had to stay elevated for the first eight. It was awful, I was on two different types of strong painkillers every four hours, I would have to set my alarm throughout the night to keep myself topped up, otherwise the pain would be unbearable and if I wanted to go to the toilet from my lying position on the sofa with my leg up, I would have to hop to the stairs, go up on my knees and get back down on my bottom all as quickly as I could because any length of time longer than a few minutes of my leg not being elevated my toes would turn blue and my foot would painfully throb with a heavy biting feeling all over. So, as you can imagine I was in a lot of pain, extremely uncomfortable and I had to rely on others to do everything whilst I lie there tormented to just watch, I hated it. I was profusely grateful, but I just hated the uselessness of my situation, not being able to help with even the smallest of tasks. I was mad really, I should have been revelling in the break from all the housework, except it just wasn't me.

My mum and sister would pop over every day and have a potter around, my family and close friends would take turns to bring the kids to and from school, to make sure I had a drink and packed lunch for the day and then pop back to put on the dinner if Justin wasn't home in time from work. The support was immense, but it was hard, and I felt like a huge pain in the arse to everyone, but I was super grateful for all their help. That was the first stressful situation I found myself in. The second came by the way of an unexpected phone call two days after I came home from the hospital. My mother-in-law, Heather, had been admitted into hospital a couple of weeks before. She had diabetes and her big toe was turning black, so they kept her in and monitored her whilst the body did what it had to do by slowly cutting the circulation off. Every time I visited, I had a slight undercurrent of anxiety that I would be standing beside her bed talking, when all of a sudden, a black shrivelled zombie-like toe would fall out from underneath the covers. It was pretty unnerving, but she handled it so well. The kids and I would all visit her almost daily, eventually give in and wheel her outside so she could have a cigarette then she would insist the kids wheeled her in her hospital chair to the nearest vending machine so she could spoil them rotten with treats. She had been apparently getting better, but complications arose and two days after I came home, she suffered a heart attack and passed away. It was so hard to register. One moment she had been chatting away on the phone requesting a KFC dinner, the next she was gone. This was the kids first death in the family that they would be forced to experience.

Understandably, Justin was distraught and totally broken. He didn't know how to process his grief, so he buried his head in the sand and refused to talk about it, allowing the sadness of losing his mum to eat away at him and for a short while I lost him while he struggled to make sense of it all. I had to grab him before he was totally lost to the dark depths of grief and the bottom of an empty pint glass. Meanwhile I also had to be there for the kids, to try and help them make sense of something even I didn't know how to even begin to explain.

My sister brought me home some leaflets on bereavement specifically aimed at children to help them understand death, but they were only thirteen, eleven, ten and eight. Their world had just came crushing down around them, how could they possibly make sense of how their nanny could be there one minute, getting better, smiling, and asking for a cheeky KFC to be snuck onto the ward, then gone the next. I'll never forget the moment I had to gather them all around me and tell them that Heather was no longer with us. Their little faces in that moment will forever be etched into my mind, simply pure, raw sadness, and confusion. I didn't want to let them go. I hugged them all close to my side for as long as they allowed.

I guess it would have possibly been emotionally easier for me if Justin had been with me at the time, but he was in no place mentally to see the kid's devastating grief, he couldn't even accept his own. We used to visit my in laws every day to walk the dogs and have a cup of tea in the build up to her going into hospital, the issue with her diabetes beginning its slow blockage causing the lack of circulation, so for the kids it was like losing the one part of the day that they looked forward to the most. Whilst visiting Heather in hospital there was one thing that we used to love doing, we all loved the movie Tag and on a couple of occasions if the hospital corridors were empty, we would recreate the final scene by me surprising them by calling quietly

'TAG'! the kids would run ahead laughing and I would have to catch them.

If anyone ever came into view ahead, we would all instantly stop and walk normally like nothing had ever been going on, on one occasion we got a smirk from a passing nurse around a corner who had caught us. It wasn't exactly sensible behaviour in a hospital environment but for those few short moments it took the concerned frowns off their faces after saying goodbye to their nan and allowed them to be carefree, mischievous kids again, just for a short while. I honestly think she thought that she might actually be home in no time. Sadly, it wasn't to be. At the time I thought I cried, showed them that it was ok to be emotional but later I learned that I hadn't been so successful and that was something they remembered, not in a bad way, in my mind I was just trying to be the strong one, but this was what forced me be more open with my feelings about how I felt with the Bells Palsy.

So, quite literally from my sofa in the horizontal position I was grappling with trying to care for my entire family. I refused to allow myself to cry or even allow the sadness to creep in even just a little, as I had to be the supporting rod my children and my husband needed. The last thing they needed was for me to break down as well, that's how I saw it.

Shortly after the funeral my son who was around eleven at the time really struggled to cope with the loss of his nan. In order to make sense of her death his brain rewired itself and heartbreakingly he started to show signs of OCD and anxiety. I first recognised something was wrong one evening when I was watching the tv whilst ironing, he was sitting at the table doing some homework and he apologised for something that didn't require an apology, initially I thought nothing of it but in the space of a few minutes he had apologised a handful of times, but didn't seem to be able not to, like he was compelled to apologise constantly.

This progressed into compulsive behaviours including touching things repeatedly and a health anxiety to sneak in and grip hold of his rational brain. I could understand to a degree where that one stemmed from. One minute his loved one was there, the next they were just gone. This transpired from concerns over his own health to a terrifying fear that something would happen to me.

This was the beginning of him needing much care and help. the year after losing Heather I had to pull him out of school as he was really struggling. He had only started senior school a couple of months prior to this so it was having a huge impact on his day-to-day life. I found this utterly heartbreaking. I could not make him all better, this wasn't a sore knee that could be kissed away or a bad dream that a hug would ease, this was serious mental health, and I felt like I was slowly drowning, unable to know what to do or how to help him. He needed constant emotional support. I was worried every single day; I had never seen anything like the signs he was showing that were manifesting from the anxiety, he refused to believe he deserved to be happy so would break apart his army model kits that he loved to build and even ripped up a cushion that he really liked on the end of his bed. Losing Heather hit him the hardest, when he did go back to school in year 8 the OCD was so intense that he would spend a seventy-five-minute lesson just trying to get past writing the date, but every time he wrote the date, he would put a line through it and write it again as it didn't look perfect enough. Luckily, we found a really good therapist from St Luke's, and she helped him begin his slow journey on healing from this crippling mental condition. He battles his anxiety and OCD like a champ. He still struggles every day. Sadly, the anxieties that he copes with have increased and taken on new forms, but he never gives up. It's been a long road for him to help his brain and heart heal, to help him guide his way through recovery one day from his health anxiety amongst others and his, at one-point, crippling OCD. But he is amazing, and he always finds the strength to manage it. There is nothing harder for a parent then to watch your own child struggle with seemingly the simplest of things and there is absolutely nothing you can do to help. Grief is a powerful emotion that affects us all in very different ways.

Thirteen

The third stress factor to come into play, like I needed anymore, was in the form of a mum at my kid's school. We weren't close but we were friends of sorts and had spent the occasional coffee morning together with a mutual friend. Before my operation I had agreed to help this mutual friend organise the leavers party for our children that were in the last year of school, this was my sons who had been really struggling with his mental health so it was important to me to make this as special as I could.

Being totally sofa bound, as remember I couldn't move from the lying position I was propped up in, but not wanting to let her down, I called multiple venues, helped put posts up on the Facebook site about what ideas were being thrown around, hunted through eBay for gift ideas and alongside my friend we left it totally open for anyone who wanted to help, to jump in at any point. This person in particular took a dislike to what I still don't actually know, I can only assume it was because she wasn't specifically asked to help out in the beginning, even though it was open for all to contribute as a team effort to give our kids the best leaving party we could muster. Their year group had been together ever since their reception age, and they were a great close group of kids. On the Facebook post threads little messages would pop up here and there that were clearly not happy and aimed at me, but I tried not to overthink it and carried on.

The result ended with some very nasty private messages sent to me through Messenger, harassing me with nothing but grief about what I wasn't doing, even though I had just had a major operation and was helping my entire family deal with the grief of losing our loved one. In general, I shy away from any kind of conflict, it makes me very uncomfortable, but I point blank refused to not attend the after party as my kids always come first and I even caught some slack from just sitting at the table with my leg clearly in a cast. I was in agony that night as I couldn't put my foot up and it was swollen the whole time whilst my crutches were propped up beside me. Looking back, it was all so petty. I completely cut this woman off and did not give her the time of day afterwards but at the time the nasty hurtful messages that were sent literally had me hiding in the bathroom sobbing my eyes out, ugly, gasping sobs that I was trying my hardest to keep quiet so as to not upset the kids, namely my son in that year group. That was the final straw I think that my mental health needed.

Except I didn't get the comeuppance from it all until the following November. Clearly going back to work after thirteen years was the proverbial straw that broke the camel's back. Maybe my brain was still processing all of that trauma, if that's the right word. Even though I enjoyed my job, I was never totally at ease, it was a daily routine for me to try and remember to adjust my right eye whenever I smiled, to squint it just enough that it matched the left which was pulled tighter by the bell's palsy. In the colder weather I would have to ask to go inside as my face wouldn't work properly, it would go numb and I would find it really hard to talk, add to that the leaky eye and I think it was just the push my brain needed to send me over the edge. For my brain to send me the message I clearly wasn't picking up on to take a break.

I persevered through and four months into having my massages and acupuncture I was starting to really see the old me again. I had total confidence that I was going to get my face back and was starting to feel that everything that the doctor from the ENT department told me was going to happen, wouldn't. I would say by the time covid 19 really started to make itself known I was maybe ninety eight percent back to being me again.

Then lock down happened.

Claire Rowden

Fourteen

Like everyone else in the world, anxiety reared its ugly head. Days were spent in a cloud of doubt and never-ending worry, hounding questions like what this horrible virus is, and dear God I hope my family makes it out alive plagued me daily. Myself and my husband would never normally watch the news, I found it to depressing and most times it actually made me feel rather helpless to all of the devastation happening around the world, but now every single day we would switch on the daily briefings and listen to the horrors of what was happening to people all over the world, we would sit on the sofa taking everything in that was being said whilst at the same time feeling that constant trickle of fear, an undercurrent that makes you want to grab your children and run and hide till it's all over, whilst simultaneously pretending that everything is ok and everyone is safe inside of our four walls. I felt the added pressure of constantly keeping on a neutral mask because the kids were also quite often sitting in the room with us, not entirely understanding everything that was being said so watching us to gage our reactions and how we reacted so they could judge for themselves how bad it was.

We didn't allow the kids to leave the house to begin with, only myself and Justin would go out to do the food shopping and even then, it was only when absolutely necessary. I had cleared out the linen cupboard in the smallest bedroom in preparation when rumours had started to fizzle from person to person that we could be about to go into a lockdown. I'm not sure I entirely believed it was going to be as bad as some people were making out but at the same time I didn't want to be left wanting, so I started to gradually collect tinned and jarred foods, obviously like every other manic person I hoarded toilet roll, every trip out I would buy a packet just in case we ran out. It became slightly obsessive to keep the cupboard topped up and all in order, looking back I guess it was a controlled distraction for myself.

I dreaded going out and whenever we left the house my chest would gradually begin to feel tighter and tighter the longer, we were out. Whilst in the supermarkets I would quite literally feel like I had an elephant sitting on my chest and on a couple of occasions where people were not respecting the social distancing rules I would have to leave and get myself outside, gasping in the fresh air to wait out the growing panic within my chest whilst Justin finished the shopping. Of an evening we would all go over to the field, which was literally just behind our house every night so the kids could get some exercise and fresh air, even though we were in a wide-open space all by ourselves, whenever the odd person did walk by with a dog or another person, I would instantly get anxious in case they came to close. As for the shopping, it would all have to be laid out onto the kitchen counter; the packets and cans sprayed with disinfectant aerosol spray. The same went for the post that came through the front door. It was also sprayed and placed into a basket to the side for twenty-four hours, then moved into another basket to indicate it could now be touched.

Both my husband and I were nervous and scared daily. It was during this period of having to stay in and constantly feeling like I had an elephant companion squatting on me wherever I went that I started to notice my face was feeling weird again. It was around the mouth and eye that I was beginning to feel a tugging sensation whenever I smiled or laughed, which wasn't often so I noticed it more. I went to the mirror in the hall that was hung above the coats one afternoon and pulled some faces to see what was going on. What I saw scared the life out of me and confirmed my fears. Instantly my brain started working on overdrive, I was so terrified that everything I had worked so hard to fix, emotionally, physically and financially was coming back to haunt me.

With all the stress of Covid, trying not to make sure the kids understood the situation but also not trying to scare them, the general pressure of trying to keep us all safe, and being fearful daily for my family meant that my face had taken a step backwards and was pulling the corner of my mouth upwards and my eye to close slightly. I was utterly heartbroken and totally paranoid that I was going to revert back fully to what I was before. There was literally nothing I could do about the changes that were happening to my face. I couldn't stop myself from stressing about everything outside of my control whenever the outside world collided inside our home and no amount of trying to take deep breaths and calm my anxiety would stop how I felt every minute of every day. I walked away from that mirror and continued with my day, resigned to the fact that what was going to happen, would happen regardless of whether I wanted it to or not. It was yet another thing that was out of my control.

Claire Rowden

Fifteen

In October that year Covid finally caught up with our house. Out of all of our family we were the first to go down with it closely followed by my siblings' families and parents. Having to go back into work whilst the country tried to figure out a way for children to manage the new way of life, I was put onto a shift rota. One morning I was at work wiping down the tables preparing for snack time whilst the children were outside playing when I noticed I was getting very out of breath, I certainly wasn't overexerting myself, so I knew there was no reason to be getting so puffed out. I spoke with my class teacher and promptly left to go home and book in a PCR test. The following day my results came in, I was positive alongside my daughter. I was freaking out, all I kept thinking was what if my face was triggered and fell again, what if we have to go into hospital and be put on a ventilator, it was a really scary time and as the days went past my husband also tested positive with one of my sons. Thankfully, a few days in we realised we were not that bad and considered ourselves very lucky, all around the world people were dying or going into hospital and we were only suffering with temperatures and shortness of breath. We felt lucky and very thankful. Daily I facetimed my parents and siblings to check they were coping ok, constantly dreading the worst, especially for my dad as has an underlying lung condition so my daily paranoia and fear for them was high.

To begin with it was Justin who suffered the most. He could hardly talk as when he did he was struck with uncontrollable coughing fits, which ended up with an ambulance call out just to make sure his blood oxygen levels were not too low, I on the other hand was seven days in and felt like I was on the turn for getting better, my face had come away relatively unscathed, surprisingly considering the stress and fear that bubbled beneath the surface and the kids were all ok which was a huge relief. Then came day eight.

For four days straight I couldn't get out of bed. I could not eat anything, could barely keep water down and had a constant wet cloth on my head to try and ease the constant pounding headaches. The only time I wasn't sleeping was when I forced myself up to go to the bathroom.

Before we all knew it Christmas had come around again and yet again, I was about to have another odd Christmas. Due to the Covid restrictions everyone was in their own homes, keeping safe and Face Timing their loved ones. Normally I would be heartbroken at not being able to see my family at Christmas, especially my husband's aunt and uncle, who we met up with every Christmas eve to share food, open gifts and just enjoy the season together. There was talk of them coming down and standing outside to see the kids, we are their only family on his aunt's side, so it was important for us and them. But I could not bring myself to agree. Inwardly, I felt awful. I knew how much it meant to them; they are more like grandparents to our children rather than great aunt and uncle. But I just couldn't cope with the possibility, and I also couldn't verbalise to them just how bad I was feeling, about not allowing them to come and mentally in my own head. The anxiety I was feeling by this point was all but taking over and it was a daily struggle to keep it hidden and appear normal to everybody. The affect that everything had had on my face was too hard to bear and it affected every aspect of my mental day to day routine. The thought of them both coming and just standing at the end of the path to see the kids created such an intense fear within me. I wasn't allowing anyone to come close just in case, my irrational brain fully taking over and I was terrified that they could have the virus without them knowing and somehow that passing to us. Like I said it was entirely irrational, and I wish I had acted differently now, but then I just wasn't in a well enough place to think rationally regardless of how it may have seemed.

Christmas is such a special time of the year and my whole family person love getting together and celebrating but this year I was grateful we were stuck at home. Don't get me wrong, the day itself was lovely, I pottered about cooking dinner whilst Michael Bublé played on the Sonos speaker, Justin and the kids pottered around in the lounge, then we all sat around the table and shared a delicious dinner together. It was beautiful, and I didn't have to worry about trying to join in with any conversation so I wouldn't look rude whilst keeping one side of my face turned away to distract from the fact that it wasn't working as it should, hiding every bite of food behind my hand because I was paranoid how I looked when I ate.

Christmas that year yet again you wouldn't find me in any photos.

The Sadder Side of Me

Sixteen

As soon as the nightmare of lockdown eased and we were all allowed to start to tentatively making our way back out into the world with each other again I called my acupuncturist and booked myself back in for treatment, determined to get back to where I was before, and I was full of a confidence that it wouldn't take that long, I mean, I had been through the worst and came back from that awful place, granted it was hard work but I had done it, so as you can imagine I was feeling pretty confident.

As usual it was booked for a Friday so my mum could come with me (Fridays were her only day off from work). Just like before, we were taken straight through, and I explained how my face was reacting. I had the needles put in all the usual places, feeling like a pro at playing pin cushion this second time around, but afterwards the doctor explained that it wasn't my face any longer that was the issue, it was my head. I needed to get help mentally because that was what was causing my face to react and pull tight. I was completely thrown off. My first reaction was to try and convince him I felt fine, and I was a little annoyed that he couldn't see that it was my face causing the issue not me but when he asked how I felt about my face on a daily basis, and after getting the look from my mum to be honest, I explained how every day, all day I thought about how I looked to other people.

Whenever I was in a conversation with anyone I would be listening and saying all the right things, but in my head, the entire time I would be worrying over whether they could see the differences in my face as I talked. I would scan every part of their face to see if I could find the mirror image of how I felt, ugly and weird looking. If I could, I would avoid eye contact and when I found something funny, I tried my hardest not to laugh or smile to much as I would really feel the pull then, and I was constantly paranoid, even around family and friends, my brain never got a break from worrying how bad I must have looked. On the odd occasion when someone said or did something really funny, I would turn my face away or try and discreetly cover myself with my hand.

They were and are the times I most feel like a vulgar, twisted gargoyle. Without realising it I literally just backed up everything he was trying to say.

I left there feeling distraught. If the problem was in my head, then I couldn't see anyway to sort that issue out. I went back a couple more times, but he said to me the problem was not anything he could fix any more, in his opinion my face was fine, it was my mental health that was causing my problems, and that wasn't something he could help with.

After years of my sister gently dropping into conversations that I would really benefit with speaking to a therapist, I finally caved and asked her to help me find one, figuring I should try and take the doctors advise. The lady we found lived close by. We chatted over a couple of calls, and I was booked in for the following Thursday evening. When I arrived, I lingered for as long as possible before I got out of the car, I was very nervous, as much as I am the first to recommend someone reach out and get the help they need, I also have the thought that no one would want to hear what I have to say. And what would I say anyway? I did however take this opportunity to let my son know that I was also seeing a therapist, to show him that a lot of people reach out and accept a little help from time to time. To also show him that he wasn't alone in this world where anxiety was, at times all-consuming. Anyway, I went up to the door and knocked.

The lady who answered was friendly and welcoming, we went into the front room of her house which was set up as an office. It was a small but welcoming space, with an open fireplace on the left-hand side, some toys in plastic containers just to the right and an old fashioned worn brown leather armchair positioned beside the window. Once I had taken my seat, she positioned herself opposite and begun to ask me some questions about why I was there and what I wanted to get out of the sessions. I only went about three times before lockdown was put back into place but in those three sessions, she helped me realise that many of my control issues and fears with my children were very probably linked to my traumatic years at school. Almost all of my memories from my school years are unhappy, in fact they are the unhappiest memories from my childhood that I have. My earliest being towards the end of junior school, that's when I started to realise that being quiet and not standing up for myself was going to cause me no end of issues. Rachel was one of my close friends, we were only around nine or so at the time, but we hung out a lot at each other's houses after school and got on well. That was until she decided one day that she didn't like me anymore, she punched me hard in the stomach in the corridors by the pe storage lockers at lunchtime and told me she was going to fight me after school. Hurt and upset I walked away off to the toilets. What I didn't realise was that she had told every other kid that she was fighting me also. I only lived up the road and would walk home on my own as it would literally take a few minutes each day, yet that day it felt like a million miles away and completely out of my reach.

When the bell went and I walked out of school I stopped dead, the entrance to the school had a long path heading towards the gate with a low wrought iron fence that ran around the school grounds separating it from the residential street and car park outside. What I saw literally froze me to the spot. Almost every child in my year was leaning forward in anticipation against the length of the fences, all in a long line with Rachel in the centre, blocking the exit. Everything slowed down in that moment, I can still see myself standing there on the beginning of that long path not knowing what to do. I no longer heard the excited squeals of the smaller kids, excited to be going home after a day of schooling, it was as if my feet had been cemented to the spot, the thought of walking anywhere near those kids filled me with such dread that my insides turned to jelly, and my body responded by physically shaking. They were all there eagerly waiting to see her beat me up, and I knew she would, she came from a rougher family then me and she had already hit me that day. I wanted to cry but my body was not reacting, I looked like a baby dear caught in the headlights of an oncoming vehicle, unable to move and get to safety. In that moment it truly felt like I was standing there looking at the nasty smirk on her face whilst trying to take in why my peers were all so eager to see me get hurt.

Luckily for me a mum saw what was going on, walked up to me and asked if I was ok, she smiled and gently took my hand and led me back inside the school. What's weird is I remember all of that situation so vividly as if it was yesterday, yet I can't remember how I got home that day, whether I eventually walked alone or whether my parents were called to come and get me. Either way it was my first experience of what was about to become my daily life in my not-so-distant future, I had no idea that things could get worse then that terrifying ordeal.

A year or so later I moved up to my local senior school desperate for a fresh start, it wasn't to be. I was bullied terribly for around five years, and I cannot recall one day of happiness in that place. I wasn't a confident and outspoken girl, I only had a couple of friends but I would mainly keep myself to myself and whenever the inevitable daily dose of abuse, both physical and emotional was due to be dished out on me by whatever girl fancied having a laugh at my expense that day, I just let it happen, too frightened to stick up for myself, which was absurd as my dad had shown myself and both my siblings how to handle ourselves if we ever needed to.

But no matter how much you are shown how to fight back or told to say the right words to make them stop, if you haven't got the confidence in the first place then it just doesn't help, well for me it didn't anyway.

This was why I never told my parents what was going on. In my mind I didn't want to disappoint them, not that they would have been disappointed in me, they are not, and never have been those type of parents, but I personally felt like a huge let down and if I'm totally honest I was also embarrassed. Both my sister and brother could handle themselves if ever anyone decided to give them grief, I just wasn't the same, I didn't have it in me. I was too afraid of the outcome, I always had this same recurring dream that I would be in a fight with an unknown girl, but unlike in real life, in my dream I always stuck up for myself but whenever I went to punch the bully everything would slow down and I would move in slow motion, which would only affect me, the other girls would stand there and laugh, then inevitably I would wake up terrified from being so badly attacked in my dream. This is what always prevented me from fighting back, always choosing to go home rather than confront the bully who was threatening me on that particular day.

The daily torrent of abuse wasn't just limited to school hours. There were a few occasions when it would spill out into the evening also. One girl came and knocked on my door after school, I knew her and we were somewhat friendly but upon opening the door and her saying hello, before I could respond she leaned forward and slapped me really hard in the face, then she laughed and ran off across the road to join the other girls who had just stood and watched. I closed the front door and went back to doing whatever it was I was doing; I didn't say a word to anyone. If I had just gone to my sister and told her what had happened, I don't doubt for a second, she would have gone out there and given the girl a well-deserved slap back, but I didn't want that, then I would have to face questions which would inevitably follow, and I wanted to bury my head back in the sand and pretend it wasn't happening. The same went for another evening, all of our dustbin bags that had been piled down the side of the house for collection the next morning had all been picked up and dumped on to our doorstep. I pretended I hadn't seen who had just run off laughing and put them all back along the side of the road.

On an almost daily basis I would go home for lunch and watch a movie like Grease, with its high school fun and friendships to encourage me to go back to school. It would never last though and eventually I got to the point where I would forge notes from my parents to regularly absent myself, or just skip school altogether. I would leave the house in the mornings and then wait in the bushes down the side of my house for my mum to leave for work so I could sneak back home for the day. Anything but to be in that imposing school where I was constantly balancing on a knife edge, never knowing if the day would be a good one and I would be left alone or if it would be like almost every other day, awful. Obviously skipping school and faking notes from my parents wasn't going to last forever and there was more than one occasion when I was caught out, either by being seen by my mum whilst she was on the school run picking up my younger brother or when my parents were called into the school, sat down in front of the head of year and passed two different sets of notes before promptly asking if both piles were written by them. I was put on report for truancy more than once and my parents must have just assumed I was one of those kids who, I assume they thought was naughty and just didn't like school. But that wasn't me, I wasn't that type of kid, and I hated that they probably thought this of me. I loved school, especially History and English, they were my favourite lessons. In hindsight if I had just told them what was going on then maybe things would have turned out differently, but that's the beauty and curse of hindsight. Or as I like to say, coulda, woulda, shoulda. It's ironic really that one of my favourite books from when I was a child, and the only book I kept in my memory box all these years is Charlotte's Web by EB White. It's a story about two friends, a spider called charlotte who tirelessly fights to save the life of a pig called Wilbur. Charlotte never asks for anything in return and Wilbur happily ends up looking after her offspring after she dies at the end, telling them all what an amazing spider and friend their mum was. It's a story about loyalty and friendship. Two things I never exclusively had. The friends I did have were not all loyal and they always wanted something in return.

 If I was left alone, I would have done really well, I got high grades on all of my course work and actually enjoyed learning, but things came to a head when I was in year ten, I no longer wanted to cope with being called all the names under the sun, constantly trying to be invisible whenever I was within the school grounds so as not to catch anyone's attention. One afternoon during my lunch break at home it all became too much. I couldn't muster the strength I needed to mentally walk back out that door that afternoon and go back to the inevitable torture that was waiting for me. I decided I wasn't going to return to school after lunch that day. Whilst sitting in my lounge, watching Grease; my chosen movie of that day through tear-streaked eyes I swallowed down all of my hurt with the large lump that was sitting so tightly within my throat, took an entire large blister pack of strong painkillers that was prescribed by the doctor and one by one swallowed them down with my water. After taking over twenty tablets, I leant back on to the sofa and waited to drift off to sleep. I was fifteen.

Seventeen

Thankfully, my mum and sister came home from the shops just as I was feeling drowsy on the chair. My mum questioned me as to what was wrong, she could see I wasn't myself. Swallowing my shame and looking down at the floor I opened my palm and showed her the empty foil packet that sat in my hand, she instantly took me to the hospital where I was wheeled promptly through some double doors and into a medical room. The nurse who was advising me what was going to happen whilst all of the other nurses flittered about around me was curt and rude. In an annoyed clipped tone, she told me I was to have my stomach pumped. I quietly and tearfully asked if I could not have the tube in my throat and her reply was quite simply 'Well, you should have thought about that dear.'

As she fed the clear tube down my throat, my hands gripping the bars of the bed as I struggled not to gag, she proceeded to lecture me on my 'stupid mistake' whilst at the same time pouring a black tar like fluid from a large white jug down the tube that filled my throat and poured into my stomach. She wasn't very nice, but I guess she was just pointing out the obvious in the hopes that I wouldn't do it again. When I think back on those days, I am mortified that I put my parents through that. If my child did to me what I did to them I would be utterly heartbroken.

I know it wasn't intentional, I wasn't aiming to hurt them, and in that moment, I genuinely thought it was for the best as I physically and mentally couldn't cope with the constant harassment that I had no control over anymore. But it wasn't until a week later, I was sitting outside the office on the first-floor corridor of my senior school whilst my mum was inside telling the head of year that I would not be returning was when the impact of what I had put them through finally hit me. I sat there in that quiet space listening to my mum break down on the other side of the door, sobbing whilst she explained why I wasn't coming back anymore. It broke me to hear my mum so upset and the regret that I felt was immense. If I had just told them what was going on things could have been very different, but I didn't. I didn't know how to, so I dealt with it on my own. This is where my control issues stem from. Subconsciously my brain needs to feel in control which is why situations that seemingly take away my control freak me out and make me stop what I'm doing. One effect of this was whenever I drank alcohol, I only ever drank a few, just enough on nights out to feel merry and to allow the happy feeling to take over so I could get up and have a dance without feeling self-conscious, but as soon as I would begin to feel the alcohol taking hold I would have to stop and change to soft drinks and water.

It's a running joke within my friendship groups that I am always the party mum, out having a good time with everyone else but unlike them I won't be downing the shots and knocking back the strong cocktails, always keeping an eye on them whenever they get drunk and making sure everyone has a safe way to get home.

So, I don't get drunk, and I over think everything. This is my problem with parenthood. When you have kids, after a certain age you must start relinquishing control, I struggle with this. I over think every situation and inwardly panic on a regular basis. Add to this the constant paranoia about my face when I interact with anyone, and you have a constant fizzy line of stress that isn't exactly healthy. I didn't think I would be going back to a therapist anytime soon; I struggled to open up and talk about issues to begin with, but even if I do manage to then I feel like I've just wasted their time, waffling on about all the things I'm sure they don't want to hear about. I know this isn't the case but it's how I felt.

Claire Rowden

Eighteen

So, where am I today. If you were to meet me on the street you would most probably not guess that there was anything wrong, or that anything had ever happened to my face. I'm becoming an expert at balancing out my right side to match my left, look a little closer and I'm sure you will see what I feel if we talk for long enough. That's how I feel on the inside anyway, regardless of how many times my friends and family tell me otherwise. To me, the difference between my right and my left is just as prominent as night and day. I will always be convinced that you can all see from the outside what I feel from within.

Don't get me wrong, I am very grateful that my face is the way it is, as I'm fully aware it could have been a lot worse. I had severe facial palsy, and I've managed to bring it back enough to be somewhat hidden, that said, I still worry daily about how I look and in turn I also still regularly try to keep myself in check with my stress levels. I can eat and drink regularly now and all my taste buds have come back,

the only obvious things that inhibit my day-to-day life
are little things like blowing up balloons, that's not so
easy, blowing out candles and whistling is also a trifle
tricky and not successfully maintained so I avoid
them if I can. In the winter my face doesn't really
work, the nerves go numb with the cold weather
which means if I stand outside for any length of time
then I can't really talk properly, and I can feel my
face slowly losing responsiveness, this also causes the
nerves to ache which can be quite painful around my
ear, so I avoid being outside in the cold for long
periods of time.

It tends to creep up on me quite slowly, one minute
I'll be standing outside watching my son play in a
rugby match, feeling cold but no more than everyone
else who has gathered around to watch their child
play, an hour later I'll be standing in the bar
afterwards surrounded by chatty rugby mums all
discussing the game at length whilst the boys all sit
together and have their after match meal and I'll feel
my face begin to slow down, that's when I know I've
gotten too cold. My face is no longer responding
properly. This really embarrasses me, I instantly try to
bring whatever conversation to a close and then take
myself off and keep myself to myself, carefully
sipping my coffee whilst listening to everyone else
chat around me. My friend Leah was my saviour in

those situations, I only have to find her, give her a look and she understood in that unspoken moment that I wasn't ok. I would stand next to her from that point on making it look like I'm part of the conversation, but she would pick up the slack and take over, knowing I didn't want to join in any longer. This was however totally unavoidable when my oldest best friend Deb made big secret plans to totally usurp my fortieth birthday and treat me to a picnic in the park. I had made it clear to all my friends and family that I didn't want to celebrate my birthday with anything special, I was turning forty and this to me was not something I wanted to celebrate.

Firstly, because I felt that was an age where I would feel officially old, and secondly because in the same year as turning forty my youngest was also going up to senior school. I would be one of those mums who had all her children in senior school so would be pegged in the older bracket. No one had said anything of the sort to me, this was all my own doing and if I think about it enough then really, it's just another reason for me to lose a little more control, my kids were growing up and needed me that little bit less, I hated it. Don't get me wrong, on one hand I couldn't wait to see the men and woman they would become but on the other if I could keep them small and by my side, safe with me then I would.

Most women would be itching to get more time to themselves, revel in the freedom that eventually comes with having older ones, but not me, if I thought about it too hard and to long, I would begin to feel a hard lump within my throat and tears pricking the corners of my eyes. The thought of them growing that little bit further away from me, needing me that little bit less and becoming more independent, which obviously I want, is also something I dread. It's so hard to try and explain without sounding like a total weirdo.

Anyway, of course everyone ignored my pleas for a very dulled down birthday, my house and my car were trashed out the front by my mum, sister and Deb with balloons and banners that let every passer-by who glanced over know my impending age, and on the inside the kids had done exactly the same with Justin. The number forty was literally everywhere I looked!

Covid was my friend that year, because of the restrictions no one was allowed to come round and visit which was gutting on one hand but on the other a huge relief as I wouldn't have to worry about making sure my face balanced up every two seconds from smiling or to run through the endless reel in my head of how I looked as I thanked and accepted presents. I've always hated being the centre of attention, so this worked perfect for me. Deb on the other hand had other ideas. She said to meet her in the park for a social distance walk so she could give me my present. When I arrived, she had taken over one of the benches and completely filled it with gift bags full of presents, balloons, and a small bottle of prosecco with two waiting glasses. I was completely blown away, it was such a lovely thing to do but it was when I opened the first gift that my hand shot up to cover my face; she had found an old photo booth picture of the two of us around the age of fifteen, the type that had four pictures in a strip, she had framed it along with some cut out sentence's from the letters we used to write to each other. It was the silliest thing, yet so amusing, when we were kids, she used to come over to hang out, we would put on a video tape in my room and watch a movie whilst chatting. Deb would inevitably shift down to the floor at some point so I could play with her hair whilst the movie was on and whenever one of us had to leave the room, we would use a lined piece of a4 paper, fold it up concertina style and with a different coloured pen each we would take it in turns to write down a sentence or two, then fold it over so it couldn't be seen and pass it over for the other one to do the same. The end results were usually hilarious as the sentences never really corelated with each other but in the same way made exact sense.

The letters she had used were from when we both liked a couple of boys and we talked about when we were meeting up with them, as well as singing lines to our favourite Backstreet Boys song. Whilst I read this the tears pricked the back of my eyes, and my heart swelled with emotion. It was such a beautiful thing to do and it meant the world to me, yes in that moment I had my face hidden as much as I could without drawing attention to it because I was paranoid about how I was looking whilst trying to keep my emotions in check but I would not go back and change a thing about that day, regardless of how I felt on the inside I would feel it again a thousand times over to live in that moment with one of my oldest friends.

The Sadder Side of Me

Nineteen

There wasn't a single day when the bell's palsy
aftereffects didn't plague me. Odd sensations that
used to happen when I would lay down at night and
try to go to sleep were among the most frustrating.
My head would hit the pillow and in order to be able
to relax into sleep I would have to make a conscious
effort to relax my face on the left side. This consisted
of taking deep breaths and slowly exhaling, with
every breath I let out I would try to relax the nerves in
my face a little bit more, and I could physically feel
my face unclench as I did it. If I didn't do this before
I went to sleep my face would feel taught like that
side of my face is suspended, frozen still in halfway
between a smile. My mum always knew if I had
either had a late night or if something was wrong
because my face would give me away every time.
I've never been a great sleeper, but a few late nights,
a few early mornings, which would inevitably lead to
me being overtired would result in my face appearing

visibly tight. I quite often would splash cold water onto my face when I first wake up in the mornings just to wake it up and make it feel less tight. If I got to stressed out my face also pulls tight, this makes my mouth in the corner not work properly so it doesn't move as much as the other side when I'm talking, which in turn makes my eye pull tighter. This, I found out is called Contracture in the face and Synkinesis in the eye. I've learned lots of new words I never knew existed before since researching this book. Neither feeling is very comfortable and despite it feeling hugely noticeable to me, on the outside it isn't as bad as it feels, well that's what I am constantly told anyway. I'm not yet convinced.

To name another annoying left over trait is I can never be to overly expressive on my left side, if I do the nerve that runs from the base of my ear and along my jaw line jolts me with a wave of pain which lasts a few minutes, it's very annoying, especially if I'm trying to get some food out of my teeth with my tongue or if I bang my little toe on the corner of the door frame and my face twists up in that agonising pain that seems to last forever, the nerve twangs and I'm rewarded with an extra painful ache in my face as well as my toe for a few moments.

I think the most annoying out of them all though has to be my eye, it has what's called crocodile tears.

Basically, its faulty wiring of the nerves that causes my eye to water, a lot. Especially when I'm trying to put on my mascara in the mornings, I must repeatedly dab at my eye with a tissue because otherwise it would be a constant trickle of tears, or if it's any kind of wind outside, again the leaky eye would be constant. In the summer I would actively avoid eating ice creams and lollies, every time I would attempt to suck on the dessert of my choice, my left eye would be pulled quite tight and my eye squints almost to the point of closing, plus my mouth still cannot purse properly so I can't suck on the ice lollies anyway, it just results in an embarrassing sucking noise if I try to hard. These are the little things that really bug me because in the summer when we are having a lovely family day out and we all decide to stop for an ice cream, I can't join in. It just wouldn't be worth the paranoia of trying to eat and look normal at the same time.

Recently, Myself and Justin went out for dinner with our cousin and his girlfriend. Just a meal to catch up and see their new house that they had recently moved into. We had such a great night. The food was amazing, the wine delicious and the company perfect. Except throughout the entire meal I was hyper aware of my facial responses whenever I had to reply, especially as I was sitting opposite them both and in close proximity. No matter how hard I tried to relax, there was the constant underlying current of anxiety gently nudging its way through my brain whenever I had to respond to something that she was saying. Justin discreetly messaged me at one point to remind me to look at her when I responding as I wasn't really making any eye contact, it wasn't intentional, but I found it easier to look at his cousin across the table next to her as the distance between us was that little bit further away.

I felt awful that I may have possibly made her feel uncomfortable or ignored, so I did my best to hold eye contact for the rest of the evening, so you see even a simple pleasant evening out for a meal is actually hard work, not that I'd let on to anyone that I was struggling because I want to go out with friends and family, I want to enjoy meals and have a laugh over a restaurant table, so it's easier to just keep it all to myself, that way I don't make people feel concerned, or worse uncomfortable enough to not invite me so they don't make me feel guilty for making me uncomfortable. It's a double-edged sword every time I go anywhere. I get all the excitement of going, I don't consider the issues that could arise during the evening ahead and like any normal person going out somewhere all I can think about is what a good evening I'm about to have and what to wear, yet when I'm there it slowly creeps in and it's like I have a gremlin that sits gently to the side of my brain, subtly pointing out all of the things that make my facial differences apparent to everyone around me.

Part of being a book reviewer means that I am lucky enough to be invited to publisher events alongside other book bloggers. I recently went to a book event in London. I met some fellow bloggers on the way, and I was super excited, especially as I was one of the bloggers that had been nominated that evening. We arrived at the venue, and it was so great, I met lots more bloggers, event organisers, publishers and more importantly the author of the book I was chosen to represent. To say I was excited and having a great time would have been an understatement. Then I saw him. The photographer organised to take pictures for the event. At that point the dread started to seep in, all the anxiety and self-doubt that had been hidden away brought rushing back to the forefront of my mind. I didn't even want to win at that point knowing I would have to go up and speak in front of everyone there and knowing that when I get embarrassed, I grin and grinning and talking doesn't exactly work so well with my face anymore.

The venue wasn't exactly huge, it was a small book bar, beautifully quaint set on a quiet street in London. As you walked in the bar was to your left offering wine, cider tea and coffee plus many cool bookish totes any bookworm would love, move a little further in and it would take you up a few steps to the back which had wall to wall bookshelves selling all kinds of books, surprisingly not in any genre order which I loved. We browsed the books with a glass of red wine for a time whilst waiting for the venue to begin, all the while I was ignoring the large upright screen to the right-hand side of the room that displayed every five slides the image of my face and the book nomination I was chosen for, it was just a little too large for my liking.

I played my part, took some selfies with bloggers and authors, posed with others when asked to by the photographer and smiled as best as I could, but the initial excitement of heading to London and being nominated for the Book Blogger awards for one of my favourite Greek Mythology books was tarnished. When the evening was coming to an end, I made my way to meet Justin who had been waiting to pick me up, climbed in, sat down, and regaled him with the evening's events. My phone made a couple of pings, so I took it out of my bag and was shocked to see the pictures that were being posted already with myself tagged in them. Every single photo taken with me in it I hated. I hated the way my face sloped when I smiled and how everyone else looked so natural, yet there I was trying so hard to look normal and all of my bell's palsy was evident for the entire world to see.

Justin tried to reassure me, told me my demons are my own worst enemy and that I looked lovely. It didn't matter though, no matter what he said it wouldn't have changed the fact that I sat with my head turned away looking out of the window secretly crying. I promised myself that night I would have to practise a new smile, the one I have used my whole life that was genuine and lit up my whole face to show how happy I was just won't do anymore. I needed to practice a more subtle smile that hid my bells better, it wouldn't be difficult, I'm used to being hyper aware of every facial expression around people by now. Needless to say, I never used my photos on social media that evening.

One of the downsides to having accounts for my blogging on TikTok and Instagram etc sometimes ill comes across a reel that has someone talking into the camera with half a paralysed face. I find this extremely triggering and traumatic. I have to swipe up or switch off, not being able to watch. The sight of anyone in person or online that has bell's palsy symptoms I will actively avoid. I think this resonates with me far too much, reminding me of what I looked like.

Claire Rowden

Twenty

It wasn't long until the government started rolling out the Covid vaccines. When these were being made available, I was thrown yet again into complete turmoil. I knew I would be offered one as I had gone back to working in the school but stupidly, I had googled bell's palsy and Covid vaccine to death and I had come across quite a few linked cases of people who previously having had facial paralysis, after a couple of days into the vaccine suffered partial paralysis again. These studies were from all over the world and even though there was no direct link with the vaccine and bell's palsy, it just hadn't been around long enough. I was convinced that I shouldn't have it. I knew I seriously couldn't go through having half of my face totally gone again, mentally I don't think I could have coped with that. But I was constantly in conflict with myself, one part of me told myself that it's better to have bell's palsy temporarily again then to die, alone on a hospital ward from Covid, to the other half convincing me that I had survived having Covid quite bad so what were the chances of getting it again.

In the end I agreed to have the Pfizer as it wasn't a live vaccine, and the results showed better prognosis. Still on the day of the jab I was seriously scared and totally convinced that I would wake up back to square one again.

I didn't of course and so far, I have had both of my jabs and even my booster. In the end I decided I would much rather have half a face and watch my children grow up then the alternative. Apparently, I read that every ten years there is a chance it can come back. I have no control over this and if it does, I've resigned to that fact that I'll just have to deal with it when and if the time comes. My only fear is that I won't be able to make it come back to the degree that I have now as my nerves never fully healed in the first place.

I once read about a man that suffered from bell's every single year for about ten years, every time he got it, it was mild enough to only last a few months and it would then completely go away again. This could be seen as a positive, after all if he can get it every year for ten years and manage to come back after every single episode then why couldn't I? but mine was never mild, and the damage left over to my nerves was severe enough to leave me with enough concerns to think that if they were affected again then how could they recover if they never fully recovered from the last time? I tell myself all the time that I just have to monitor my stress levels and make sure I take time out for myself on a regular basis if I feel it all becomes too much, I never really put much importance on self-care, but I do now. If I'm honest though this is probably through fear rather than the health benefits to myself. Despite all of my attempts to control my own anxiety I'm still not very good at it.

I eventually had to leave my job at the school. I was signed off for six months with stress. I wasn't coping and my face played a huge part in that. I planned to go back but eventually I had to leave to take care of my eldest child. He was really struggling with school and being in his last year I needed to help him with his GCSE's. He suffered from social anxiety and struggled to be in the school so we would go every morning and sit together in a side room whilst he worked and then come home in the afternoons to continue his revising at home. He was also on the waiting list to be accessed for ADHD as the older he got the more he struggled with his ability to focus and retain information.

Despite all of the struggles he had he managed to sit his exams, and he came away with brilliant grades. He applied to a college and got a place that he wanted. I couldn't go back to work as he needed me all the time and at any time of day in case he needed to come home, so I decided to use my time and began my writing journey.

Twenty-One

These days I feel I have perfected my mask that I wear. I will allow myself to be in photographs, but I tend not to save them. If it's a photo that I'm taking myself for my blog then it takes at least ten takes minimum before I get one that I'm happy with, this is when people look at it and say 'it really doesn't notice, you look great in that photo' but what they haven't seen is the countless attempts it takes me to get that 'normal look' that everyone takes first time around with a carefree snap. I also tend to offer to take the photo if we are in a group or with friends, that way I can preview the photo before it goes public. I still find myself caught unawares sometimes whenever I'm pottering through the house, I'll be walking up the stairs and my eyes will catch on one of the many photos I have lining the wall up the stairs of me doing something fun with the kids or out with our friends frozen and happy encapsulated in time. I get caught up in the memory, wishing I could go back and get that version of my face back, or googling celebrities I will be watching on television or in a movie that appear to have similar traits to me when I smile and talk just to see if they also have had this condition. It's an odd thing to do, but it does make me feel that little bit better when I read that they also have gone through something similar to me. I feel slightly more normal in that moment. I tend to think of myself in two halves now. Me before the palsy and me after.

I think one of the most irritating and regular issues I tend to have, aside from the leaky eye and the occasional painful twang along my jaw, must be the on and off paranoia of whether I have a toothache and if I need a filling or whether it's just the nerves playing up and causing a temporary ache. I absolutely hate the dentist. I didn't have a very good experience when I was younger so anything other than a general check-up tends to be done under general sedation, so the thought of having a filling, regardless of how small would always fill me with a constant dread that would bother me all day long.

The number of times I've paid to see the dentist, convinced that I have an issue with a tooth only to be told they are all fine and nothing needs doing. You would think I would put two and two together considering the tooth ache is always on the left side of my face, up the top and towards the back, but I don't, and every time it happens, I give myself the unnecessary stress and constant worrying until I build up the courage to get it looked it.

As much as I have just gone on a lot about what I feel I am left with, like I said before I am extremely grateful that I have what I have, it's annoying that the doctor I originally saw at two weeks in was in the end right all along. I did get rid of a lot of what the condition caused on my face but I am also left with significant changes, but they are changes thankfully that I feel and see personally more than others do and unless I tell you beforehand and you do not know me, then you may not even realise I'm different to you or that on the inside I'm quietly searching your face to see if you can see all of my defaulted parts that I'm desperately trying so hard to hide, whilst looking as normal and relaxed as possible.

Claire Rowden

Twenty-Two

You may be wondering what I hope to achieve by
putting pen to paper and writing my story down and
sharing all my raw and private feelings with you all?
Well, firstly I needed somewhere to begin my writing
journey, and this seemed like the best place to start.
My sister had been gently pushing me to put my
feelings and experiences down on paper ever since it
all began – probably a therapeutic technique she was
trying to get me to use - so this seemed like the
natural choice. I've always wanted to be a writer, and
this seemed the best place to start. Writing down all
of my emotions and sharing with you quite possibly
the worst things to have ever happened to me has
been extremely emotional and difficult in equal
measure, but it has also helped me in more ways than
one. The words I found just flowed whenever I picked
up my pen, forcing me to keep notebooks all over the
house and in my bag for any 'just in case' moments.

Also, I wanted to put myself out there with the hope
that someone would like to read my story and take
something away from it, to know that if they like me
were suffering and unsure of what to do then to take

hope that all is not lost. But more importantly I wanted to raise awareness for bell's palsy. I had never heard of this condition until it completely changed my life and if I didn't have the support of my family and friends around me to support me and tell me about alternative therapies then my story could have been very different. I'm not ashamed to admit I was in a very low place when this all started, I came out the other side because of the support of my family, others might not be so lucky.

Don't get me wrong, I have read that most people will only contract bell's palsy mild enough that it goes away by itself within three months of first getting any symptoms, mine unfortunately was severe and just wasn't the case, I don't honestly know if it would have gone away by itself or not, the doctor didn't seem to think so and I was not prepared to take that chance so we found a way to find the money to pay for regular treatments to try and fix me. I'd like to hope that if someone happens to wake up one morning and discover that they have a condition that scares the hell out of them, I want them to know that they are not alone and I'd like to think that maybe my book will pop up in a search engine or a friend will have seen or heard about it and recommend it to be read and hopefully it will make them realise that even though you might feel like the only person in the world to be going through something so traumatic, you're not, I'm here and I've been there. Because it's not a condition you have to just accept, it is treatable and with the help of acupuncture and massage then like me you can get back to being you again or you enough so that you can be happy. Because despite everything that I have been through, that is where I am at. I'm not content or satisfied with how I look, I have good days and bad days, good days where I barely notice I'm different, changed in a way that isn't always easily recognisable and bad days where I spend the whole day feeling like my face has been pulled so tight I wouldn't be surprised to trace my fingers round the back of my left ear and feel clips pulling my skin taught. I don't think I ever will be ok with myself anymore, but my mental health has a lot to do with that, I can't solely keep blaming the condition. I sometimes like to think that if I can sort my head out then one day my face will follow, I won't tell you my success rate thoughts on that though…

Until then I'm very grateful for what I am left with.

I'm happy enough to be happy.

Claire Rowden

Acknowledgments

I wanted to write a quick thank you to a few people, who put up with me and my paranoid ways day in and day out.

To my two best friends.

Firstly, to my oldest and bestest friend Deborah, you are always my ear if I need to rant and moan and tell me straight regularly if I'm being paranoid about how I look, also thank you for loving my book enough to burn your bacon and let your tea go cold! You are the opposite side to my coin, and I would be lost without you.

Donna, thank you for also hearing me moan and worry constantly about how I feel I look and for just being there regardless over endless coffees, you make me feel so much better about myself and you are like my twin pea in the proverbial pod of life.

Also, Leah who always had my back at rugby, ready to take up the slack when I need to slink away from conversations if I'm feeling insecure and for just knowing that I'm feeling that way by the look on my face. You are the sensible outlook on my problems when I'm freaking out, and the Thelma to my Louise.

I wouldn't be able to write an acknowledgement page without saying a big thank you to my biggest fan Hayley, whether we are walking around the lake getting some exercise or chatting over the phone you always encourage and push me to take the next braver step whether it's with my blog or my books and always the first to cheer me on.

To my first ever bookstagram friend Emma, you have been supportive all the way through and at our latest book launch event made me feel very special after telling almost everyone we met how I had written a book and how amazing it is. Thank you for giving me that glow.

Lastly, saving the best for last, there are not enough thank you's in the world to make up for the gratitude I owe to my family.

Dad, thank you so much for being the first to read my completed first draft and for giving me some great feedback, your opinion was the one I wanted most and it filled my heart so much when you told me how much you loved it and that I had a talent for writing, also for always encouraging me to read whilst growing up, I would not be the reader I am now if it wasn't for you.

Mum, thank you for endlessly coming with me to all my sessions, holding my hand and never once making me feel like a pain in the bum. I genuinely could not have got through all my sessions if you were not by my side, but mainly just thank you for being you, I truly did get the best mum in the world.

Kelly, it was you who first gave me the idea to put my thoughts down on to paper and encouraged me not to give up, I don't honestly know if I would have even been brave enough to start writing this book if it wasn't for your words of encouragement. You have been the sensible sister sitting on my shoulder and

always there if I ever needed any advice or support.
Thankyou.

Richard, thank you for making me realise there was
an alternative solution out there and for your constant
support.

To all of you, thank you to the bottom of my heart for
propping me up, keeping me going and making me
feel always like I was as normal as the rest of you.
Well, our kind of normal anyway!

And finally, saving the best for last, to my husband
Justin and my children Jack, Alfie, Harry, and Molly.
You are my life. I love you to the moon and back and
without your endless unconditional love, cuddles,
kisses, and unwavering reassurance I don't think I
would have made it through. My cup quite literally
spillith over.

I love you all.

What Is Bell's Palsy

Bell's palsy, also known as idiopathic facial palsy, is a form of temporary facial paralysis or weakness on one side of the face. It results from dysfunction of cranial nerve VII (facial nerve) which directs the muscles on one side of the face, including those that control eye blinking and closing and facial expressions such as smiling. (There are 12 pairs of cranial nerves, identified by Roman numerals.) The facial nerve also carries nerve impulses to the tear glands, the saliva glands, and the muscles of a small bone in the middle of the ear. The facial nerve also transmits taste sensations from the tongue.

Bell's palsy is the most common cause of facial paralysis, although its exact cause is unknown. Generally, Bell's palsy affects only one side of the face; however, in rare cases, it can affect both sides. Symptoms appear suddenly over a 48 - 72-hour period and generally start to improve with or without treatment after a few weeks, with recovery of some or all facial function within six months. In some cases, residual muscle weakness lasts longer or may be permanent.

Because the facial nerve has so many functions and is so complex, damage to the nerve or a disruption in its function can lead to many problems. The early symptoms of Bell's palsy may include a slight fever, pain behind the ear, a stiff neck, and weakness and/or stiffness on one side of the face. The symptoms may begin suddenly and progress rapidly over several hours, and sometimes follow exposure too cold or a draft. Part or all the face may be affected. (rarediseases.org)

Symptoms of Bell's palsy can vary from person to person and range in severity from mild weakness to total paralysis. The most common symptom is sudden weakness of one side of the face. Other symptoms may include drooping of the mouth, drooling, inability to close eye (causing dryness of the eye), and excessive tearing in one eye. Individuals may also have facial pain or abnormal sensation, altered taste, and intolerance to loud noise. Most often these symptoms lead to significant facial distortion.

The cause of Bell's palsy is unknown. Stress is considered to possibly be a major contributing factor. Swelling and inflammation of the cranial nerve VII is seen in individuals with Bell's palsy.

Most scientists believe that reactivation of an existing (dormant) viral infection may cause the disorder. Impaired immunity from stress, sleep deprivation, physical trauma, minor illness, or autoimmune syndromes are suggested as the most likely triggers. As the facial nerve swells and becomes inflamed in reaction to the infection, it causes pressure within the Fallopian canal (a bony canal through which the nerve travels to the side of the face), leading to the restriction of blood and oxygen to the nerve cells. In some mild cases where recovery is rapid, there is damage only to the myelin sheath (the fatty covering that act as insulation of nerve fibres).

For individuals with new-onset Bell's palsy, steroids are highly likely to be effective and can increase the probability of recovery of facial nerve function. In most instances, oral steroids should be started within 72 hours of symptom onset, if possible, to increase the probability of good facial functional recovery. Some individuals with co-existing conditions may not respond well to or be able to take steroid drugs. Antiviral agents (in addition to steroids) might increase the probability of recovery of facial function, although their benefit has not been clearly established. Bell's palsy is an idiopathic condition, meaning that no conclusive cause has been established. Although no certain cause has been established, people newly diagnosed with Bell's palsy should understand that they are unwell. It is important to get plenty of rest even if they have no other symptoms and to maintain a healthy diet. **

Another important factor in treatment is eye protection. Bell's palsy can interrupt the eyelid's natural blinking ability, leaving the eye exposed to irritation and drying. Keeping the eye moist and protecting it from debris and injury, especially at night, is important. Lubricating eye drops, such as artificial tears or eye ointments or gels, and eye patches are also effective.

Other therapies such as physical therapy, facial massage, or acupuncture may provide a potential small improvement in facial nerve function and pain.

In general, decompression surgery for Bell's palsy—to relieve pressure on the nerve—is controversial. On rare occasions, cosmetic or reconstructive surgery may be needed to reduce deformities and correct some damage such as an eyelid that will not fully close or a crooked smile.

The prognosis for individuals with Bell's palsy is generally very good. Clinical evidence of improvement occurs spontaneously within three weeks in 85 percent of cases, and most individuals eventually recover normal facial function. Some individuals may be left with mild residual facial weakness or show moderate to severe deficits. Bell's palsy can have consequences from a previous injury or condition, such as involuntary mouth movements when trying to blink the eyes or incomplete recovery of facial muscle weakness resulting in trouble speaking or forming words (dysarthria). ***

Possible complications left over from Bell's Palsy - Due to the complexity of our facial muscles and their function, a number of problems can arise following the prolonged experience of having Bell's palsy:

• Contracture: Shortening of the facial muscles over time may make the affected side of the face appear to be slightly 'lifted' in comparison to the unaffected side, and the affected eye may appear smaller than the unaffected eye. The fold between the outer edge of the nostril and the corner of the mouth may seem deeper due to the increased contraction of cheek muscles on that side.

• Crocodile tears: This means that the affected eye waters involuntarily, particularly whilst eating. This is due to faulty 're-wiring' of the nerves during the recovery phase.

• Lagophthalmos (pronounced lag-op-thal-mus): This is an inability to close the affected eye, which if prolonged may result in eye dryness and/or corneal ulceration. (This complication can be assisted/prevented by the use of artificial tears and taping the eye down at night.) In rare cases, the vision may be permanently damaged if care is not taken.

• Synkinesis (pronounced syn-k-eye-nee-sis): This means that when intentionally trying to move one part of the face, another part automatically moves. For example, on smiling the eye on the affected side automatically closes. Similarly, on raising the eyebrows or closing the eyes, involuntary contraction of the cheek or neck muscles occurs. Find out more about synkinesis.

• People with persistent symptoms of Bell's palsy may experience psychological problems including stress, anxiety, depression and low self-esteem.**

Information courtesy of

**FacialPalsy.co.uk

***The National Institute of Neurological Disorders and Strokes. (NINDS)

For more information and helpful videos the FacialPalsy.co.uk website is very helpful and informative.

Claire Rowden

Acupuncture

Acupuncture is a treatment derived from an ancient
Chinese medical technique for relieving pain, curing
disease, and improving general health. It was devised
before 2500 BCE in China and by the late 20th
century was used in many other areas of the world.
Acupuncture consists of the insertion of one or
several small metal needles into the skin and
underlying tissues at precise points on the body.

Acupuncture grew out of ancient Chinese Philosophy
dualistic cosmic theory of the yin and the yang. The
yin, the female principle, is passive and dark and is
represented by the earth; the yang, the male principle,
is active and light and is represented by the heavens.
The forces of yin and yang act in the human body as
they do throughout the natural universe as a whole.
Disease or physical disharmony is caused by an
imbalance or undue preponderance of these two
forces in the body, and the goal of Chinese medicine
is to bring the yin and the yang back into balance with
each other, thus restoring the person to health.

An imbalance of yin and yang results in an
obstruction of the life force, or qi, in the body. Qi
flows through 12 meridians, or pathways, in the body,

each in turn associated with a major visceral organ (liver, kidney, etc.) and with a functional body system. Acupuncture is designed to affect the distribution of yin and yang in these channels so that the qi will be enabled to flow freely and harmoniously.

The actual practice of acupuncture consists of inserting needles into any of hundreds of points located over the 12 basic meridians and over several specialised meridians. The needles used may be slightly arrow-headed or may have extremely fine points. The typical insertion is 3 to 10 mm (0.1 to 0.4 inch) in depth; some procedures call for insertions up to almost 25 cm (10 inches). Once inserted, a needle may be twisted, twirled, or connected to a low voltage alternating current for the duration of its use. The physician frequently inserts needles at a considerable distance from the point on which they are to act; for example, a needle inserted into the pad of the thumb is expected to produce analgesia in the abdomen. Similarly, successive points on a specific meridian may affect widely different areas or conditions, e.g., the first six points of the yin lung meridian deal primarily with swollen joints, excessive heat in joints, bleeding of the nose, heart pains, mental depression, and inability to stretch the arms above the head. The location of the points is mastered using innumerable diagrams and models. There is speculation that acupuncture can relieve pain, including to the extent that it can act as an anaesthetic during surgery.

Evidence to support this notion, however, is lacking.
*

Celebrities who have Suffered from Bell's Palsy

So, considering Bell's Palsy affects 1 in 60 people every year, I thought I would just highlight some well-known celebrities that have also suffered from this condition. Just so you can remember that this condition isn't particular on who it chooses to affect, it affects us all.

Angela Jolie

Angelina Jolie developed Bell's palsy in 2016. She credits Acupuncture for her successful recovery.

Pierce Brosnan

Irish actor Pierce Brosnan, known for his four roles in James Bond films, suffered from Bell's palsy in his youth and has since fully recovered.

George Clooney

George Clooney, winner of three Golden Globes had Bell's palsy in middle school. That sultry half-smile is an after effect of the condition.

Katie Holmes

The former Mrs. Tom Cruise and actress from Dawson's Creek was also a victim of facial paralysis. It is thought the residual effects of Bell's palsy are responsible for her classic facial smirk

The Sadder Side of Me

About the Author

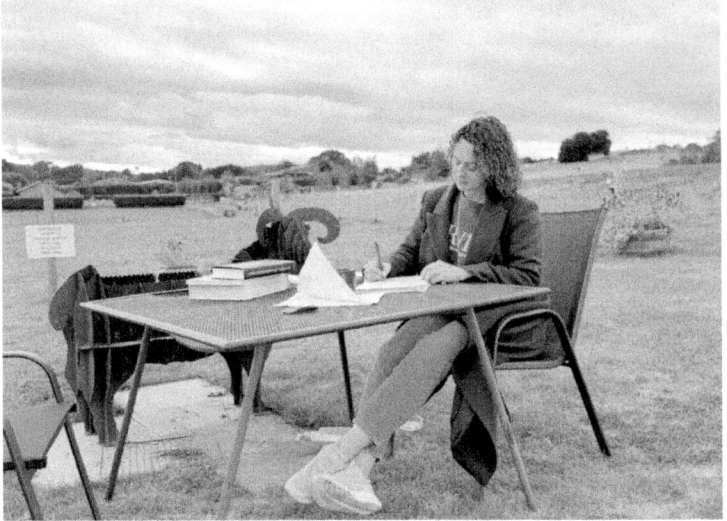

Claire Rowden lives in Essex with her husband, their four children, seven cats, and a unique quartet of Silkie Showgirl chickens. Their household is a lively blend of love and laughter, reflecting Claire's nurturing spirit and her passion for life.

Balancing family life with her professional aspirations, Claire is currently training to be a psychotherapist, driven by her deep desire to understand and support the emotional well-being of others. Her compassionate nature and insightful approach make her a natural in the field of mental health.

Claire is also an avid reader and a dedicated blogger. On her Instagram blog, Secretworldofabook, she shares her love for reading with a growing community of fellow book enthusiasts. Her blog is a vibrant space where she discusses her latest reads and connects with others who share her passion for literature.

When she's not immersed in the world of books or her studies, Claire finds solace in nature. She loves spending time outdoors, finding peace and inspiration in the natural world around her.

In addition to her non-fiction work, Claire is in the process of publishing her first fiction story, bringing her creative talents to a new and exciting frontier. Her writing reflects the depth of her experiences and the resilience she has developed along the way.

Claire Rowden

Printed in Dunstable, United Kingdom